Growth Encounter
a guide for groups

Growth Encounter
a guide for groups

Kurt Haas, Ph.D.

Nelson-Hall nh Chicago

Library of Congress Cataloging in Publication Data

Haas, Kurt.
 Growth encounter: a guide for groups.

 Includes index.
 1. Group relations training. 2. Small groups.
I. Title.
HM134.H16   301.18'5   75-2180
ISBN: 0-88229-225-0

Manufactured in the United States of America

For A.R.J.

Contents

Preface

While encounter is much discussed and has had a great deal written about it, no book has detailed clearly the procedures involved. As a consequence many groups are led by people who are well-meaning but essentially uninformed. People who are interested in leading encounters or just want to know what goes on have had to depend upon scattered sources or throw themselves naively into a group situation. It is not surprising, therefore, that much of what passes for "encounter" is a disappointment or worse.

This book tells how an encounter is conducted, step-by-step and in detail. Every vital technique and application is explained in straightforward, nontechnical language. Questions of those experienced in encounter and those new to it are answered: Who can benefit from encounter? How useful are games? When are anger, physical contact, and confrontation appropriate? Whether the reader is interested in encounter as a professional, a student, or a participant, he can use this book to help create a productive encounter experience.

In addition to serving as a source for those who want to take part in or lead groups, this book explains a particular kind of group interaction—*growth encounter*. Growth encounter groups emphasize the help individuals can give one another through intensive mutual understanding and concern. Encounter members help themselves (and one another) to overcome inhibitory barriers and maximize their capabilities. Growth encounter is neither psychotherapy nor counseling for the distressed; it is an intensive personal interaction designed to help individuals explore their own lives and enlarge their experience.

Chapter 1

The Purpose of Growth Encounter

Intensive group interaction, whether called encounter or something else, is a social phenomenon nearly without precedent. In little more than a decade it has reached into education, business, institutions, and families and has touched the lives of millions. Why? Because people have found encounter can relieve their loneliness and stimulate change. Encounter can enable individuals to break out of their monotony and, perhaps for the first time, really recognize themselves and others.

However, not all encounter groups are worthwhile. Groups led by the unskilled (no license is required to lead groups) or groups that hint at sensational experiences frequently leave their participants considerably disappointed or even seriously upset. In order to be productive, encounter must be an informed and purposeful experience. Participants should know their goal and feel comfortable with the methods they will use to get there. All groups need not be headed by professionals,

1

but any person assuming directional responsibility should be thoroughly knowledgeable, practiced, and trustworthy.

Encounters may be beneficial and valid without being directed towards growth. The movement to help individuals change by encouraging them in relationships with others has a fairly long history that has resulted in some very diverse sorts of groups. Many groups, particularly those called "T-groups" (T for *training*), deal primarily with interpersonal conflict situations. People in the same office or neighborhood may be brought together in an attempt to help them resolve tensions and open new avenues of communication. Other groups, like the Tavistock Programs, may focus on the group process itself, requiring members to work out their own procedures and act together to reach their objectives.

Still other groups make use of very specialized techniques or unique definitions of their ultimate goals. Psychodrama requires that participants act out roles almost as if they were part of a theatrical company. Gestalt encounters develop very intensive interactions and are often led by psychologically trained specialists. Sensitivity groups tend to emphasize the here-and-now; participants try to help one another increase their awareness of all that is happening around them and within them.

Different from all these groups is group psychotherapy. While all encounter-type groups try to promote some individual improvement, psychotherapy has treatment as its specific aim. Group psychotherapy may be psychoanalytic, client-centered, or based on some other treatment approach. But its core is the fact that people have been brought together to help them recover. Such therapy interactions are for people seriously in need of care, and as long as they need such professional help they are not likely to benefit from any sort of encounter.

Encounter is for relatively healthy people, with at least minimal adaptive resources, who want to get more from their own lives and to enlarge their experience. Growth encounter, like other encounter-type relationships, is aimed at helping the person bring out or maximize his capabilities. It is a group experience whose aim is to stimulate self-development. Growth encounter is based on the theory that when people get together and respond honestly and openly to one another, emotional and intellectual knots are loosened. In the growth encounter, the understanding and encouragement of others helps the individual give up some of his defenses and recognize repressed feelings and capabilities. He is helped to overcome the social pressures, fear, guilt, and self-doubt that may have forced him to shut off his capacity to experience and mature. All those present are intent on re-exploring their own aptitudes, continuing their growth, and actualizing their potential.

The Participants

Those who seek encounter for growth and can benefit from it represent all age brackets, occupations, and backgrounds. Any adult regardless of education, ethnic background, or social status can participate with profit. But those who profit most from the experience tend to have certain personality characteristics. Besides wanting to grow and explore new facets of their character, they are relatively thoughtful, fairly patient, and cooperative. They want to know who they themselves really are, but they also want very much to share affection and feeling with others. One encounter member put it very well when she said, "I want to feel my own humanness and share the humanness of others."

Incidentally, I am aware I am using inexact, nonscientific terms, but I am being neither deliberately vague nor poetic. Much of encounter is feeling, sensing, and intuiting; words do not easily describe such happenings. Perhaps an indispensable quality in potential encounter participants is an ability to let themselves feel and be comfortable with sensations and events not readily communicated by words. One test of how well prepared a person is for growth encounter might be his reaction to the following statement. Near the end of a series of sessions, one growth participant said, "I don't know if I am different, but I feel different." I suspect that those who can empathize with this statement rather than finding it too mentalistic, introspective, or personal are likely to be ready for encounter.

It may be best to let encounter members speak for themselves. Here are some excerpts from early sessions, when participants frequently talk about why they came and what they expect. Though some discontent is evident in every self-description, each also shows a very positive motive to "become more."

> I am 28 and right now I'm not working but I've been a teacher. . . . What brought me here I guess is that for years I've just been tremendously bored. . . . I found I was locked into routines. Just playing a role. I read the women's magazines, watched T.V. and I was just copying the role as they defined it. I was playing at being mother, wife, homemaker, and it was so unoriginal and so monotonous. . . . I mean for a while I just believed that life was supposed to be boring. I mean I just came to accept boredom. . . . That really shook me. Surely I can be more . . . that's what I want to find out.

> As a social worker I enter the lives of others. Well I suppose it would be the same if I were a doctor or a lawyer or even a foreman or something blue-collar. Anyway it hit me that I was so busy in everyone's life that I never really thought about my own. . . . One of the people in my case load kind of startled me. . . . He made me think. I was rushing them or something, or being bossy, and they came back with something like do I ever stop playing social worker and act myself. And all along I thought I was being very human but I started to think maybe I wasn't. . . . So I began to see that maybe I was always being the social worker and never myself. Then I saw that maybe it was easier for me that way. I needed my job as a cover, almost . . . maybe. I thought maybe if I didn't have my job I would be terribly lonely, I would feel awfully lost. . . . I had the usual things, friends, supposedly, marriage . . . a decent salary but I was still terribly isolated. My life touched lots of others but I had no intimate friends. There must be people I can feel at home with and

completely trust but either I haven't found them or I haven't found what's holding me back. . . .

I'm here because I'm curious about what's happening in other people's lives. That is, I want to know myself, whether what I am doing and feeling makes any sense, or like the questions I have about marriage and careers and such. How do other people handle this, what do they think of what I'm doing. I want some sort of background against which to know what I am doing and judge my direction. . . . People ordinarily, even your wife or husband, or your parents or anybody, people are not that close that they'll really help you to see yourself. . . . Maybe you might call what I feel self-doubt, or maybe I lack confidence or something, but I feel I can't judge that on my own. I want the help of others. I want perspective on my own life.

The Group

Growth, however differently it is expressed by individuals, is the final objective of encounter. But unlike physical or even some intellectual development, which could be an isolated activity, personal progress occurs through interaction with others. We learn what we can do, our limits as well as our abilities, through the eyes of others. Parents, siblings, or other relatives may initiate the process of self-definition. Later playmates, teachers, and friends all play their part in creating our understanding, our image, of ourselves. In the encounter group that self-image is reexamined. Now each person has available trustworthy fellow humans who want to help him overcome his negative perceptions and advance his capabilities. The encounter participants all listen earnestly to one another, exchanging thoughts, feelings, and insights. They each give sustenance and support and encourage new goals and behaviors. Ultimately whatever psychological growth occurs in them will be a result of what they and the group have learned about, and taught, one another.

The group interaction needs to be brought to the fore since its give and take is the heart of the encounter experience. What each can become may lie hidden within him, but getting there is hugely dependent upon the dynamism within the group. However, the group situation is not created solely for the development of any one individual. No one has eight or ten others working diligently on his "case." What he gets from others is counterbalanced by at least two contributions he makes himself. First, he tunes in very carefully to the rest to determine how he can help. At the beginning he learns to give full attention to others and devote serious thought to their condition. Eventually he gives the individuals in his group all the concern, understanding, and affection that he himself might need. He is there to help and he works hard to do so.

The second contribution a person makes in the encounter comes from the modifications he begins to impose on his own behavior. Many of us may have been aware that what we do and say affects the lives of others, but frankly we may not have cared a great deal about it. At its worst this attitude is expressed as "I'm me, and to hell with the rest." But no one will get away with being oblivious to the needs of others in encounter. In the microcosmic, intensified world of the group anyone can see, and may be told directly, that what he does and even feels has a very real impact on all around him. Others may never have commented about his aggressiveness, or may have been too intimidated to point out his negativism. But in encounter these traits cannot, will not, and should not be overlooked. The members will let him know how his aggressiveness or other traits affect them, and he may be compelled to evaluate just which of his own characteristics stand in the way of growth—for others as well as for himself.

All we do affects others, whether fellow worker, neighbors, children, girlfriend, or husband; we need to adapt some of our ways to meet their needs and expectations. In encounter people get a chance (which may eventually benefit those they live with) to give up habits and behaviors or learn new attitudes and responses to meet their healthy requirements. In the words of an encounter member who once fought long losing battles with himself because of a false sense of individuality, "Encounter gives you a chance to come to terms with yourself as a living and needed part of the lives of others."

A very serious misconception about encounter has spread—the notion that in encounter people are urged to do whatever they please, almost any time and anywhere. Perhaps there actually are such group situations, but this kind of whim gratification is contrary to growth encounter theory and is discouraged. Liberating every fragile impulse, hoping to satisfy every urge and fantasy, does not put one on the path to self-actualization. Those who believe psychological progress lies in following whims are not freeing themselves but actually imposing a new straitjacket. A person responsive only to his own needs is a captive of impulse, a prison just as confining as the most sterile routine imposed by an unsatisfactory job, marriage, or personal shortcoming.

A tendency to follow what may turn out to be fruitless impulses may arise even in growth encounter, particularly in the middle stages. Sometimes as old inhibitions melt away momentarily enthralling opportunities seem to emerge. Novel ambitions and drives appear, beckoning enticingly. Now at last, participants may be convinced, they have found themselves. If encounter stops at this stage, or if the group relationship has not developed sufficiently, a participant may mistakenly believe himself finished. He thinks he no longer needs the group, for he has been able to free new desires within himself and is impatient to begin his adventure.

But it is at this stage that the group is really needed most. Now its presence serves as a reality check. Each member needs the concern and understanding of others, for at this point others may be in closer touch with his potential than he is. Here is Chuck's* description of such an experience:

> It was around the ninth meeting, as I remember, that I came to the group all fired up. I was going to be a wandering troubador. Get in my car, pack my guitar in it and everything I needed and head West. Goodbye Millie, goodbye job, good-

---

*The names of participants and all other identifying data have been changed to insure confidentiality.

bye Ned and everybody, goodbye. I mean the folksinger thing
had left a real mark on me. You are completely free. You eat,
you wander, you love and man, you are free. . . .

Now by this time the group was really into each other. I
mean they were not my family or anybody and making fun of
me or anything. They liked what I said. They said they liked
my spirit. I think my enthusiasm was catching and they caught
some of it from me. So we all really thought together about
what I was going to do. None of them ever said don't do it or
ever seemed doubtful. But then as we all felt this thing through
together, we started remembering some of the other things I
had learned and this troubador thing started seeming to dead-
end. I wanted to write. And really for the first time I had
started very deep relationships and it meant a lot. And I was
just beginning to experience myself. . . .

The more thought we gave it the clearer it became. The
wandering folksinger thing was actually a kind of way to really
say "No" to my own progress. . . . Too many people do that,
you know. They find out a little bit on their own, or in a
group they learn a little about their insides and then they go
off half-cocked never really exploring the depths. . . . You
can't be free, till you know what is really going on, deep,
deep, down inside.

Encounter is a freeing experience. People find themselves
bound less and less by frustrating conventions and life-negating
restrictions. But they will not emerge from encounter led
astray by egotism, diverted by impulse, and callous to the
needs of others. In a good group they will have had their negative attitudes discouraged and positive ones reinforced. Their
fellow participants will not have let them get away with behavior, good or bad, that outsiders might tolerate or ignore because they were too unconcerned or confused to say anything.
They are not taught mindless conformity to group expectations.
Individually, a person becomes more himself in encounter. But
in a growth group his self-development occurs in a social context; his maturation is a joint product of his own needs and
those of others with whom he exchanges insight, affections,
and respect.

The Process

Growth encounter, like other group interactions, evolves through several stages. At first members feel uneasy, confused, and perhaps even suspicious. In this initial stage they often question the usefulness of the whole enterprise and wonder about their own and others' motives for being present. Given a little reassurance that doubts and anxieties are common to all, the participants usually begin to feel more comfortable. Most members then describe past feelings and present ambitions but do so fairly carefully, since they are not yet sure how much to trust others. But as more and more participants speak up, a sense of good will and genuine concern seems to develop which leads to more honest revelation, and vice versa.

In growth encounter the atmosphere of good will, of thoroughly honest and altruistic intention, is an indispensable part of the group process. Increasing trust brings with it a good deal of profound self-examination along with candid personal reactions to the needs and characteristics of the other members. All sorts of once-hidden disguised and repressed traits and wishes may become obvious and be discussed. But at no point will growth encounter become an acrimonious, accusatory confrontation. Very serious, perhaps even provocative discussions will take place, but they will occur in a milieu characterized by acceptance, good intention, and genuine affection.

Many have the impression that encounter is a pressurized mini-courtroom with members accusing, cross-examining and shouting. While this behavior may characterize some groups, it is contrary to the growth process. When the guidelines suggested in subsequent chapters are followed, soon after the members have achieved a minimum of comfort with one another the group experiences an almost visible climate of what the eminent psychologist Carl Rogers calls "unconditional positive regard." The members affirmatively like one another, they fully accept each other, they do not need to put each other down, and they want very much to help.

In the climate of warmth and openness many of the feelings released first are fairly negative. Participants live again all the sad, burdensome, and restrictive emotions they may have long suppressed. They reveal some of their innermost doubts and describe all the bad and deprecatory emotions they have about themselves. What they seem to be doing is taking advantage of the climate of care and acceptance to purge themselves, getting bad feelings off their chests. This catharsis may last quite some time, actually taking up many if not most encounter sessions. But once freed of negative and disabling emotions, members can let positive feelings emerge. They become alerted to new ideas, drives, and potentials they may never have considered before. They no longer feel drained and diverted by useless anger or frustrated by the unattainable. Their new understanding moves them forward and their newfound needs and potentials help them feel alive.

This summary does not imply that encounter proceeds at an orderly pace with members just sitting back waiting for growth. Group meetings do not follow a script. Participants are at different levels of insight and actualization, and there is a continual forward and backward flow. Also, despite the obvious atmosphere of friendly concern, the meetings themselves may not be very polite or decorous. Someone may cry, show anger or enthusiastic joy. Members may sit or stand or sprawl, for informality is as indispensable as openness, warmth, and spontaneity.

At no time are all members equally self-fulfilled and free of anxiety. Nearly all will continue to feel anxious now and again, for they are continually working to understand themselves and to communicate with others. Most important, peeking inside ourselves, breaking through inhibition and repression, is not a very comfortable procedure. Many of us are afraid that if we look too deeply all sorts of wild and unmanageable motivations may be released. After all, we have probably been taught all our lives to hold ourselves down. We have been warned continually that unless we inhibit and deny we will become uncontrollable predatory animals. Thus throughout encounter, no matter how much people think they have learned to trust what is inside them, they continue to experience a good deal of discomfort and uneasiness as they seek to become known to themselves.

All of us admittedly have some fairly uncomfortable emotions hidden away. We do need some controls, from traffic lights to well-defined felony statutes. But the evidence suggests that what most healthy people repress is not so much an evil impulse as it is nearly the opposite. Carl Rogers, Abraham Maslow, and other psychologists have shown that what is hidden (and can be uncovered in growth encounter) is likely to be essentially good. If the repressed seems bad it is only because so many of our healthy needs, our most life-affirming motives, have been warped and distorted by punitive parents or a negating, authoritarian environment. When freed of destructive guilt and hostile defenses, as Rogers firmly believes (and the evidence from valid encounter demonstrates), actualized people reveal themselves as wholesome, productive, and loving.

Encounter ends after twenty or thirty sessions, as previously agreed, with nearly all participants experiencing some measure of self-fulfillment. Not all members stay till the end. Legitimate reasons may persuade some to leave; in addition to scheduling difficulties, some may not be ready for such an experience or may find their psychological adjustment too fragile for encounter. Good encounter does *not* end with every member deciding to divorce, change jobs, move, or become an encounter guide. The "success" of some encounters has been described in terms of marriages dissolved or emotional breakdowns occurring as a consequence. Encounter may result in such drama. But I am almost inclined to rate a group a failure if radical life changes take place as a result of a beginning relationship.

Some modifications and new behaviors may result, for some people, following a valid growth situation. But it is not essential that everyone alter his life. For most participants a worthwhile encounter results in happier attitudes, some new expectations, and the discovery of a few once-unsuspected capabilities. Perhaps even more important, while many members may not really act very differently, it is almost a hallmark of a productive growth encounter that at the end they "feel different."

Limits and Results

Growth encounter is not, and cannot be, group psychotherapy. Those with poor mental health or associated difficulties require treatment; they will not benefit from encounter. This does not mean that those once ill are forbidden encounter. After suitable treatment and with the consent of their doctors, many with formerly serious adaptive problems may well gain from a growth experience.

Just as encounter is not intended to aid those with serious emotional problems, it should not include those with severe personal crises. The man depressed and suicidal because his wife has peremptorily left him should not join a growth group for relief. The purpose of encounter is not to provide friendship for the depressed or counseling for the bereaved. However altruistic their motives, those who give such assistance should do so outside a group. An encounter is a very special situation limited to those who want to deepen their awareness and emotion and reactivate their growth. Such people need to be at least relatively healthy and fairly free of really serious life problems—though all of us face at least some difficulties. Including a truly disturbed person in an encounter helps neither that individual nor the group.

Bart's wife had left him very suddenly and without warning. The only hint at what was coming was that about six months before, following a very serious argument, Bart's wife had gone to Chicago to live with her sister. She stayed for two weeks, during which time Bart pleaded and begged on the telephone every day for her to come back home. Finally he threatened violence to both her and himself and she relented. The past six months Bart and his wife had seemed to be getting along, but obviously their basic difficulties had not been resolved. After Bart's wife left him again, leaving only a note that she was never returning and could not be traced, Bart seemed totally lost. Because he was so depressed, mournful, tearful and at a loss for what to do he was asked to come into a "sensitivity" group that had already met twice.

During the first meeting people listened sympathetically as Bart poured out his complaints and accusations. He was obviously enormously burdened with guilt for what he believed were his own shortcomings. The group listened with compassionate interest and some voiced considerable support. During the next meeting Bart and his story, and the members' attempts to console him, also took up nearly the full period.

In subsequent meetings Bart returned over and over again to his marital tragedy and his morose feelings. The other group members became increasingly less sympathetic. Many felt that Bart was beginning to waste their time; they had come for a personal experience and not to act as Bart's counselors. Ultimately some members tried to divert Bart from his story, and some even became critical of him for feeling so sorry for himself. By the seventh meeting impatience with Bart had reached such a pitch that some group members, hesitantly at first but then very plainly, suggested Bart leave the group. Bart had remained very agitated and depressed throughout the seventh meeting and when asked to leave became extremely angry, shouting obscenities and storming out. Later that evening he committed suicide.

In addition to being inappropriate for the mentally ill or those experiencing a crisis, encounter is not the answer to every life problem or frustration. It would be a mistake to hope that simply participating in a group could make a dull, uninteresting career or marriage exciting. Further, not everyone is prepared to sacrifice the time and energy a growth group requires. Some people want the entertainment of encounter but not the work; they cannot muster the dedication. All of these problems are minimized if encounter participants are informed and know what it is they are to experience. Consequently every encounter should specify its limitations as well as its objectives, state individual responsibilities clearly, and suggest frankly who might and might not benefit.

While not all participants demonstrate obvious changes in behavior, nearly all members report that they carry away new feelings and insights. They see themselves as more spontaneous, creative, joyful, and genuine. They believe their lives less restricted by inhibition and fear and uncover all sorts of potentials which can only be described as self-actualizing. But do these feelings last? The little research that has been done is not overly encouraging. Investigations have pointed out accurately the inadequacy and even potential danger of many spurious groups. But even worthwhile encounters do not seem to produce uniformly positive and lasting changes for everyone. Once outside the group, confronted again with many of the harsh limitations and stubborn realities of their everyday environment, encounter members seem to lose much of the positive momentum of their experience. Too many really good participants who have taken worthwhile steps within their group seem quickly to shed every gain they have made.

It is not really surprising that a relatively short encounter experience has limited enduring impact. The growth encounter described in this book, like other one-time group interactions, is just a beginning situation. Those who make progress in such an elementary group should, perhaps, go on to groups that will reach deeper and be more demanding. Those who do go on are very likely to carry over more and more from encounter to their everyday existence. Thus while a first encounter may not have dramatic or long-term benefits for everyone, for nearly all it can be a beginning in the process of self-fulfillment.

Another reason I am optimistic about valid encounter is that in my experience, very often human character is not readily measured. Much of what we experience and learn, in our everyday interactions with others or more formally from a book or teacher, has only a tiny incremental effect on our behavior. Our life plans and styles are seldom if ever altered in an immediately observable way by any experience, however good. But if we look carefully, we often find that minute alterations have occurred, shifting our direction. Apparently encounter results in such minute incremental changes. Good group relationships seem to plant seeds which often germinate much later, culminating in a wide variety of growth.

In addition to benefiting individuals, encounter may bring worthwhile cultural change. In his book *Beyond Words* (Russell Sage, 1972), Kurt Back has noted that some behavior scientists have called encounter the most important social innovation in centuries. They see a shift away from cold rationalism and mindless competition to a considerate society with members in close rapport, aware of one another's needs and requirements. This kind of idealism has motivated universities, foundations, and individuals to create huge encounter-type institutes designed to influence large numbers of people; they hope that somehow the goodwill and harmony within good groups will transfer to the world at large.

Unfortunately, I doubt whether encounter can bring about major social improvement. The openness, warmth, and concern of growth groups are not likely to replace the hostility, fear, and ill will characteristic of so much of our environment. Despite its rapid spread, encounter has involved relatively few people, and of these only a minority have been in situations meaningful enough to help them change permanently. To expect such small numbers to have an impact on the whole world seems far too optimistic. Further, those most in need of the benefits of encounter—those who are domineering, suspicious, intolerant and restrictive—are the least likely to participate voluntarily. Thus I must admit that I have hope, rather than expectation, that encounter will change society. But I have every realistic anticipation that for many individuals encounter can stimulate growth and help them be more spontaneous, loving, fulfilled human beings.

Chapter 2

Participants and Setting

Encounter participants should be relatively healthy both physically and psychologically. As pointed out in the previous chapter, those with serious difficulties do not belong in encounter and instead frequently require specialized professional help.

Participant Characteristics

The best participants are those who are curious, willing to enter new relationships, and motivated to work. Many of us are used to being passively amused. We watch sports, movies, and TV and become accustomed to sitting back, doing nothing, while entertainment is paraded before us. This attitude is evident in many students. They attend class and watch the teacher blankly as if they were viewing television. If asked to participate in the class—to discuss, contribute, or think—they are almost at a loss for a response. So too in encounter. Very often participants say they want the experience but then simply watch what goes on and remain aloof. They want to experience encounter vicariously, just as they experience the emotions of a drama while sitting in their living rooms watching television.

In addition to being willing to work and contribute their share, encounter participants must have much tolerance for the feelings and needs of others. Group members do not come together in order to condemn, moralize, or chastise. Though others may act in ways they disapprove of, encounter members must at least be willing to listen without making judgments based on narrow beliefs. Those who are excessively rigid, moralistic, insensitive, or unsympathetic should not take part in encounter sessions. But are these not the very people whose attitudes should be changed? Should they not be helped to be a little more open and responsive to the needs of others? Yes. But an intolerant, authoritarian person is not likely to be helped or helpful in an encounter run by average people with little advanced training. Persons with these difficult personality characteristics can benefit from group situations that are much more structured than the average encounter, and especially those guided by a highly qualified professional.

Another person who is not likely to do well in encounter is one who has been "ordered" to attend. Sometimes a physician, spouse, parent, or even employer virtually commands someone to participate. Often a husband or wife threatens some retaliation unless the spouse attends a group. Many people do learn of encounter groups through friends or professionals and may go at the suggestion of another. But the person who is attending against his will, who is not really a volunteer, is typically a source of great difficulty. He is likely to drop out quickly. But if he remains, he does so only to be obedient; forever distant, suspicious, and superior, he ultimately drains the group by the attitude of imprisonment that he conveys.

Good encounter members are tolerant, motivated towards personal growth, and eager to take part in the give-and-take of each session. A roomful of good members can mean a positive experience for all if the group is also somewhat heterogeneous. When all group members are alike in age, job, and sex, sessions may be quite dull. A group consisting exclusively of middle-class mothers, all married and in their early thirties, all high school graduates and of the same faith, is unlikely to have a very productive encounter. Such a gathering may be ideal for very specific or topic-oriented groups, such as "consciousness raising" groups or groups discussing motherhood, but the members are too similar to stimulate the kind of interaction that should take place in encounter.

Encounter groups should be fairly heterogeneous. Here are some guidelines:

1. Age differences should cover a range of 10 or 20 years. If the group's age range is too broad the oldest member, say 62, may be called "Gramps" while the youngest, say 17, is called "Kid." Too much difference in ages, more than about twenty years, freezes roles and expectations and should be avoided. Groups whose members are very close in age, for instance all adolescents or all senior citizens, can provide a good experience, even though members' perspectives may be more limited. Such groups may be helped by having a very experienced guide who is much older (or younger) and becomes less a participant than an objective commentator.

2. Men and women should be about equal in number. If there is only one woman, or one man, that one person will be seen only as a representative. The same rule holds for such classes as married and unmarried people and parents and non-parents. There should always be more than one person of each sex and, if possible, more than one who are married, divorced, or a parent.

3. A "minority group" member should be included, but for reasons identical to those above there should be more than one. If only one member of a distinctive ethnic group is included he becomes more and more a representative, a delegate from his ethnic-cultural background, rather than just another person taking part in a total encounter experience.

4. Occupations and educations of the participants should be mixed. A group can be awfully dull if it includes only teachers or business people or any other career group. It is best to have college people and non-college people, and to mix professionals with blue-collar and white-collar workers and students.

Some categories of people should not be included—for instance, professionals who are bound to play authoritative roles. Physicians are notorious in this respect, and to a lesser extent so are psychiatrists, psychologists, and lawyers. The medical doctor in a group may be unable to leave his mask of superior wisdom in his office; he may continue to play at being the ultimate authority. Unfortunately some members may begin to depend upon this role and turn to "Doc" for definitive answers. Obviously if a physician, lawyer, or other professional cannot leave the trappings of his calling behind him and take part in encounter simply as a person, he can seriously distort the entire experience for everyone.

Two other categories should not be included in any encounter group except one formed for that very category— married couples and encounter fanatics. The married pair, or members having any equivalent alliance (even very close friends), bring to encounter not only themselves but a vast network of feelings, communications, and private concerns relevant only to their own relationship. They should not, as they nearly always do, attempt to draw the other members into the conflicts and strategies of their partnership. If they want encounter they must be willing to experience it as individuals, alone, not as a pair.

Spare us the encounter fanatic, too. He has been to the West Coast and East, hit every group in town, and been touched by every famous person who has ever written about or led groups. Such "encounter freaks" crave elements of the experience in nearly the same way an addict needs his drink or drug. They attend sessions in search of a new emotional "high," continuously seeking another alleged peak experience.

The worst aspect of their presence in a group is not that they repeatedly assert their supposed expertise but that they tend to push, pull, and prod the group to give them the "high" they need. They manipulate the encounter to give them a feeling of love or the satisfaction of a hostile aggressive clash. In the process they turn what might have been genuine interactions for the other members into events staged for the benefit of one individual.

One does not have to be an encounter fanatic, of course, to manipulate others for selfish ends. On occasion all of us have had such motives. But the individual who persists in attempts to control the group only to satisfy his own cravings may be an undesirable group member even if he is not an encounter freak. This does not mean that everyone should limit himself to one encounter. After the first encounter many participants are prepared to go further, taking part in group experiences that go far deeper and may bring very significant behavioral changes. Those ready to keep moving ahead are by no means encounter fanatics and are discussed further in chapter 11, "The Growth Experience."

The encounter fan has his equivalent in the "encounter reader." While the fan has drifted through endless encounter sessions, the reader has perused nearly everything published and knows just what to expect. Even worse, if a member seems to be departing from what the reader believes his reading has taught, he lets that member know in no uncertain terms. Like the fanatics, the readers are "pros," know all the supposed rules, and want to make sure everything goes according to schedule. Such attitudes effectively dry up the spontaneity and enthusiasm that must characterize encounter groups. One cannot follow an ironclad timetable or try to force things to happen if one hopes to develop depth of personal interaction and growth. Such self-declared experts seem to take real satisfaction in making other members uncomfortable by confronting them with statements like these: "Why don't you tell him you hate him, instead of just saying you disagree" or "You're wasting everyone's time, you haven't said a single thing about how you really feel." Neither the encounter reader nor the fanatic has much to give a group. They might be advised instead to seek specialized help for what could be a symptom of deeper personality difficulties.

Finally, guide and members should be flexible and creative! Often some of these suggestions and the procedures to be outlined have to be modified. The needs of participants and the special circumstances of the encounter may require significant innovations. For example, frequently an experienced guide dealing with conscientious participants may work quite well with an all-business-people group or may include a fan or reader as a member. Guide expertise, participant commitment, and honest enthusiasm, can sometimes compensate for what might otherwise be serious encounter hazards.

The Group Setting

The size of the group is very important and should be closely controlled. With too few members each session becomes far too intense (and possibly much too intimate) too quickly. When that happens, members usually feel too anxious and threatened to go on; the group quickly evaporates. With too many members, the encounter becomes more a formal discussion group. Many members become frustrated at each meeting because they did not have enough time to say what they wanted while others seemed more successful in making themselves heard. An encounter group of the type presented in this book should not number more than ten or fewer than six participants. Eight seems ideal. But one might start with nine members since one, maybe more, may drop out. If there are nine members and three drop out very early, say in the first week or so, it is all right to invite two new members to take their place. But after four or five sessions, it is inadvisable to bring new members into the group. At that point the adjustment for the new member and the old ones is too difficult. Too much has gone on for the new person to feel he understands or to be readily accepted by the others.

Groups should meet two to three times a week for about

two hours at each meeting. Meeting twice a week, with several days between, is probably perfect. Three times is satisfactory but a little time-consuming. More than three meetings is too intense and demanding a schedule for a beginning group experience, and only once a week is far too lax. When a group meets only once weekly, there is little intellectual or emotional carryover from one session to another. Meetings should be held often enough so that the group is able to start on Thursday, say, pretty much where it left off on Monday.

Two meetings a week, each two hours, is a lot of time. But if encounter participants want more than a superficial intellectual discussion they must be prepared to put in the work and hours that this schedule demands. Further, they should expect to meet for twenty to thirty sessions. This may mean ten to fifteen weeks of meetings. Those who consider this kind of schedule burdensome are probably not good encounter candidates, for they already show an unwillingness to rearrange their lives even a little or to expend the kind of effort that is needed to bring about personal growth.

Marathon sessions—those lasting five, ten, or twenty hours at a stretch—are not encouraged. Such prolonged and intensive interactions may be appropriate for those who have already had encounter experience, but for beginners they can be almost disastrous. Too many individuals become permanently disenchanted with encounter or even scarred and traumatized by such prolonged, fatiguing sessions. When people meet for endless hours they tend to become hostile, brittle, impatient, overreactive and vulnerable. Little long-term good is accomplished when one feels emotionally drained after such a session. In addition, one of the main advantages of sessions that continue for two or three months is that members are quite likely to integrate their worthwhile encounter experiences into everyday life. When they meet for a breakneck weekend the experience, even if good, is too isolated an event to have much beneficial impact on the rest of their existence.

No detail of encounter is too small to ignore, and thus I have definite feelings about the type of clothing that should be worn. It is important that participants be comfortable, relaxed, and casual. Slacks and comfortable blouses, shirts, and tops seem best for both men and women. This clothing enables members to feel comfortable or get on the floor and otherwise move about in ways which dressier attire may not permit. But a more important reason is that when everyone is dressed in casual sportswear, obvious signs of status, profession, and role are obscured. Participants cannot concentrate as easily on the fact that George is a minister or Helen a nurse or Jim a plumber. As much as possible everyone in the encounter should be seen as an individual, a personality, without the connotations education or income gives. Simple dress helps remove the obvious distinctions and makes it easier to concentrate on the person.

A second important reason for casual clothing is that it tends to minimize what is falsely called sexiness. Much of women's conventional attire, and some of men's as well, is intended to be erotically provocative. Such fraudulent provocation is out of place in an encounter. Therefore, just as members can minimize role cues in the clothes they wear, they can make certain that their clothes—while aesthetically pleasing and attractive—do not convey the theme of "flirt and tease" that is so much a part of our everyday existence.

Despite a great deal of foolish suspicion and spurious publicity, a good encounter is not an erotic free-for-all. In fact, just as provocative clothing is undesirable, sexual teasing, seduction, and liaisons are forbidden. I have no doubt whatsoever that we live in a sexually repressive, erotically negative, and affectionately negative society. I am not barring sexual interplay from encounter because I wish to reinforce the sex-negative, inhibitory attitudes of our environment. Quite the opposite. If members are to free their sexual potential, to liberate their physical and emotional capacity, the false, misleading games of sexual chase and titillation that we have all learned from our highly repressed milieu must be barred. There will be lots of talk about sex, some touching, and a good deal of affection exchanged between encounter participants.

But it will be honest, open, and the result of treating one another as people rather than sexual objects.

For reasons that should now be apparent, the members of the encounter group must abstain from sexual-emotional involvements while in the group. Sometimes a couple begin to be especially drawn to each other and want to meet outside the group. However commendable their motivation, they should wait till the series of meetings is over. For the benefit of the rest of the group, as well as themselves, they should put off their partnership for one or two months till all the sessions are completed. Not surprisingly, what may have appeared an almost perfect pairing after the twelfth session may be viewed quite differently after twenty-five meetings. There are many early enthusiasms, and if couples were encouraged to pair off there would soon be no encounter group but instead a morass of complicated emotional and personal entanglements. Anyone in the group who thinks he has at last discovered just the right partner should wait to see what he thinks afterwards. A 34-year-old married woman described some of her feelings in this area:

> I noticed Bud the moment the group began. He was tall, lanky, had curly hair, and seemed so casual and relaxed. He seemed very comfortable in his masculinity and yet also seemed so naive . . . almost childish. I had some very warm feelings for him almost immediately. He was so many things that my husband wasn't. . . .
>
> It wasn't really till the third meeting that we began to talk to one another in the group and I felt myself even more attracted. He and I seemed to have so many things in common. He liked what I liked. He even said he always seemed to be going out with women that were the mother type and I thought that fitted me to a "T." . . .
>
> Since we weren't to meet after the sessions I managed to walk out with him fairly regularly or I would arrive early and often find him waiting for things to start. That's how we started talking just about us. . . . It wasn't very long before I thought I loved him. He was the answer to my husband whom I seemed to care less and less about. I knew this wasn't what

was supposed to be happening in the group, or even very proper. But I also knew that you have to trust your own feelings more. I both wanted to go further with Bud and still hold back. I sensed he felt somewhat the same way although neither of us ever said directly how we felt about each other. We both knew the group was counting on us to continue with them as individuals and we both agreed we could not let them down. . . .

Well the short and sweet of it is that as the months went by my perceptions grew. I knew Bud was almost like an infatuation. I was glad the group had us wait and put off so we could see ourselves more clearly. I will always like Bud but I know now that he is not what I need or want. . . . As I've grown I've learned there is no one special man whose love will make of me what I want to be. I can only get there through myself. And those I love have to give more than I think Bud is capable of. I've come pretty far and I think he has an awful long way to go. . . . I like him very much, as much as anyone in the group. But he and I are not right for each other now.

The room in which the group meets should be comfortable, quiet, and above all sufficiently soundproof or remote so that members do not feel they are being observed or overheard. A professional office, a living room, a church recreation hall, or even a small meeting room in a hotel can be adequate. It should be comfortably furnished, with some hard and some soft chairs, so that people can sit in either or can sit on pillows, carpet, or bare floor. There should not be a table between people, since this suggests the atmosphere of a formal meeting or conference. Participants should feel free to move about, changing their seating and location.

No refreshments! Under no circumstances should there be coffee, cookies, cheese, drinks, or any other refreshments. If someone needs a drink of water he can go to get it. In some groups in which refreshments are served too much time is spent thinking about the goodies that are to come. Worse yet, if different people are in charge of refreshments then comparisons are made between last week's wine and gourmet cheese and this week's meager fruit punch. The business of encounter is difficult, all-consuming, and concentrated. There is no room for interruption by food or snacks. For the comfort of the nonsmokers, smokers should seriously try to limit the amount they consume during the two-hour session. In any case the room should be well ventilated and comfortably heated or cooled.

After the session, of course, participants can eat and drink as they please, but without having post-encounter coffee hours. As already mentioned, sexual contacts or affectional liaisons between members are discouraged. The same is true for social contacts. After meetings members may tend to "get together" in the kitchen or at some local diner and discuss what happened. This is very bad for the morale of those not participating in such discussion, and the talk is generally very loose and gossipy, with undesirable results. Hence no post-encounter coffee breaks, social gatherings, or other contacts are encouraged. During the entire length of the encounter period the participants should avoid one another socially. If they do come into contact then their interaction should be limited to the usual superficial niceties. There should not be any discussion of the encounter experience outside the designated two-hour session.

If all these prohibitions—no food, sex, parties, flirtations, coffee breaks—suggest that an encounter is a "purified" experience in which people approach one another as people without props, gimmickry, or falseness, then they give the right idea. Following the admonitions about clothing, the room, food, and socializing should help members focus on the people themselves with as little distraction as possible. This is the central theme of the interaction.

Additional guidelines may be necessary in a specific situation. For example, I was asked recently about a participant who had a few drinks before each session, supposedly to help him loosen up. He argued that in order to be open and really understand others he needed the disinhibition that alcohol reputedly provides. I cannot accept this argument. If we are supposed to focus on who we really are, we must do so without the assistance of whiskey. It should be apparent, therefore, that alcohol, drugs, and other chemicals (except those medically prescribed) are strictly forbidden. The encounter participant who insists on fortifying himself with a few drinks or getting a drug "high" should be asked to leave the group.

After participants have heard these "rules" and have introduced and described themselves (as discussed in chapter 4, "Techniques for Starting"), one or two members may not return for a second meeting. Some will be disappointed, having expected nudity or cosmic joy or having hoped to find their future spouse, since this is what some sensation-seeking news media erroneously report as encounter. Others may not want the experience, for good and substantial reasons, or may be too bigoted or distressed to tolerate an encounter interaction. Leaving the group after the first session should be actively encouraged. Guides should not retain participants who labor under misconceptions or (for whatever reason) force themselves to remain in a situation that may be dreadfully uncomfortable for them. In order to reiterate the group's purpose, and to permit people to feel free not to return if their judgment so dictates, I usually say something like this:

> Now we know a little about each other and also what to expect from this encounter. I know this may be different from what you had thought or even hoped for. But this is what will happen here and we will be following the procedures I've mentioned. Not all of us may want this kind of experience, or need it, so we ought really to think it over carefully. Between now and the next meeting we should give some very real thought as to whether we want to participate in this situation with the people we've met tonight.
>
> Let me repeat, some of you may not feel that this is what you need or want, and you should feel completely free not to return. Those who do return should have a good experience awaiting them. By working together we should be able to increase our own growth and the depth of our interaction with each other.

Confidentiality

Finally there is an inviolate rule which, though mentioned last for the purpose of emphasis, must be made clear to everyone at the first meeting before much else is said. That rule is *confidentiality*! All who participate in the encounter must pledge their solemn word that they will not reveal anything said during the sessions. While a guide cannot pass around a written contract, he should state explicitly that anyone taking part in the group makes a solid commitment to everyone else in it not to reveal what is said or done. This is not because some lurid tale of extraordinary, hidden transgression is likely to be revealed. Most people lead ordinary lives and do not harbor deep, dark secrets. But everyone in the group wants and needs to feel that when he talks about himself—his needs and shortcomings, his fears, longings, and relationships—his significant feelings will not become the subject of nitwitted gossip.

The rule of confidentiality must be total. This means that even the participant's wife or husband, lover, parent, or close friend may be told no more than, for example, "Today we talked a lot about how we got along as teenagers." Nothing more; that is, a general descriptive sentence or two may be appropriate, but no names or descriptions of any kind can be included. How long should one keep the sessions confidential? In my view, forever. Ultimately those who go on in other encounters or write about their experience may want to relate something that happened earlier. In such instances the narrator must make absolutely certain that what he discloses is so far in the past and in addition so completely disguised that no one has the slightest chance of recognizing a participant.

There is no way of enforcing confidentiality except by the harsh expedient of dropping from the group anyone who violates the rule. This must be done whenever anyone, no matter at what stage of encounter, deliberately reveals the concerns of any other member. But this severe alternative is not often necessary. Encounter members do not often gossip about one another or otherwise reveal confidences. Violations of the pledge to respect what goes on in encounter and to keep it confidential are very rare. Those sincerely motivated to move forward in their own life soon develop a relationship with others in their group that makes them want to do all they can to help. Put another way, the overwhelming majority of encounter group members develop such wholesome interactions with one another that they find the notion of breaching another's privacy totally alien and abhorrent. After all, one of the main purposes of encounter is to learn to build meaningful relationships with others—relationships based on affection, honesty, and trust.

Chapter 3

Guiding the Group

Encounter groups require a guide. I much prefer the term *guide* to leader, trainer, or chairperson because that title describes the function most accurately. A man or woman who *guides* is in every sense a participant and not just an arbiter or enforcer of rules. If the guide is distinguished in any way it is that while he is part of the particular encounter expedition, he has made the trip before. He or she is a little more aware of possible hazards, knows some of the shortcuts, and can be depended on to help the other explorers find their way. Above all, I believe, the guide's function is to keep the group members from getting hurt. Besides facilitating the development of every member and their interaction, the guide is there to safeguard all participants, since amateurs (like first-timers in any new undertaking) can overestimate their capabilities.

Ideally the guide would always be a specifically trained, Ph.D.-holding psychologist or other highly qualified professional. But the boom in encounter means that at any one time there may be hundreds of thousands of groups in the United

States; there are not nearly enough educated guides available. In addition, it is important that intelligent and sensitive lay persons, without special training, begin to play a more active role in areas touching upon human adjustment. Such non-professional contributions have already been valuable in several mental health areas; it is equally appropriate for talented men and women to take an active part in groups that aim to maximize human potential. We need conscientious lay persons as encounter guides, for there is little likelihood that the need for guides can be met by professionals alone in the foreseeable future.

However, the lay person should not attempt to move an encounter group beyond the beginning stages. Only the basics of a first encounter are described in this book; professional guidance is required when people want to move further. After a participant has made a good start on his own growth and has begun to relate more meaningfully, he frequently wants to go far beyond this initial encounter. He may want to seriously probe his marriage, reevaluate his sexual boundaries, alter his responsibilities, and in fact examine critically his entire life circumstances. Since such efforts can be very intense and often produce highly charged, dramatic encounter situations, they require the most skilled and highly trained assistance. While for the purposes of the kind of beginning encounter described here (and for most other introductory groups) a responsible nonprofessional may be a satisfactory guide, for the more advanced encounter experience a qualified psychologist or the equivalent is indispensable.

Guide Characteristics

Here are several characteristics a worthwhile guide should have:

1. Though not necessarily possessing an advanced degree, the satisfactory guide should have had some vocational experience in which he was in contact with people in a helpful way. Frequently counselors, teachers, personnel em-

ployees, clergymen, social workers, peace corps or "poverty" workers, or persons with similar experience make satisfactory guides. Their contact with people has already taught them about the needs and frustrations nearly all of us endure, and they are more ready to understand and listen sympathetically.

2. The personal values of the guide should be consistent with the objectives of encounter. Through his own experience, reading, or thinking, he should have come to believe in the importance of personal growth and self-actualization and the desirability of deepening person-to-person interaction. The guide must also be sufficiently liberated to recognize just how his own conventions and background may have been inhibitory and may bias and restrict him.

3. The guide should have a reasonably strong ego; he should not be easily offended, panicked, or diverted. He needs to know both what might be possible and what the realities of life demand. One should get the feeling that the guide is a down-to-earth and reasonable person who is positively motivated and whose aim is high.

4. The ability to listen fully and effectively, as well as to talk and communicate, is indispensable for a guide. If a guide has been good at any of the jobs mentioned under 1., the chances are that much of his effectiveness depended directly upon this ability to really hear what was being said and in turn say clearly what he intended.

5. The guide must have had previous encounter experience. Attending one, two, or even five good encounters does not automatically make the participant an expert ready to launch himself as a professional. But several good encounters may well equip an otherwise capable individual, meeting the criteria described, to act as guide in his own beginning groups.

It seems best to pause here, for the temptation to spell out all the desirable characteristics of a guide is so great that before long I would be describing a saint rather than a mere human. But there is one important trait to avoid: group members should be particularly alert to whether the guide has a special ax to grind. The guide should not let his own particular concerns or orientation determine the direction in which the group goes. More than once I have talked to former group participants who seemed to have gotten a good start with a reasonable guide only to be diverted by the unspoken agenda of the person heading the group. While sitting in on one group's meetings as an observer, I noticed that the guide continually seemed to bring the discussion around to a particular political ideology. He seemed very intent on demonstrating that nearly every member's maladjustment or conduct could be traced to the pressure of certain political and economic factors. In other situations I have noticed otherwise capable encounter leaders focusing exclusively on sex or marriage or motherhood simply because they had special interests or problems in those areas. A guide need not be a saint; as long as he has the qualities enumerated and is without special preconceptions of this kind, he may well help the group make the most of their experience together.

What the Guide Does

Whatever special thing the guide does, he should be doing less and less of it as time goes by. Put in a more formal way: the guide increasingly shares his function with the group participants as they in turn develop greater skill in carrying on the group process. Eventually guide and participants are nearly indistinguishable, for the guide participates as a person and the participants help guide one another. But it would be erroneous to think the guide is ever totally submerged. It is a kind of false democracy to insist that no one ever be other than an encounter participant. The guide will be needed less and less as the group develops, but he should always be ready to offer his special contribution based on his own greater experience and slightly more objective concern.

At the beginning of the group experience the guide's main function is to demonstrate by his own example his noncritical acceptance of the members of the group and their concerns. The guide may start the group process with some of the techniques discussed in chapter 4, "Techniques for Starting," and thereafter listen carefully, fully, and in a nonevaluative way to what everyone says. The two adjectives *nonevaluative* and *noncritical* are extremely important, for they are directly contrary to what we do continually in ordinary conversation. We commonly sprinkle our interchange with comments or facial expressions emphasizing our agreement or disagreement or judgment about what our friends are saying. Here is an example of an evaluative, critical reaction:

> When Gerald's turn came to talk about himself during the first group meeting he spoke for some time about his newly started gourmet-style restaurant. The guide interrupted and said, "Your restaurant sounds nice, but tell us more about yourself." While seemingly encouraging this was actually a critical statement, for it suggested that Gerald's description of his restaurant was not important. Gerald consequently stopped describing his new business and switched to talking about his mother rather glowingly. Then, abruptly, he was interrupted by a participant who said, "Come on, no one's mother is that good."
>
> After this comment the situation continued to deteriorate until Gerald felt impelled to say, possibly out of anger, "I think you should all know that sometimes I am a homosexual." At this point one could see the participants shuffling uneasily, several even seeming to edge their chairs away from Gerald. The process of critical evaluation of another member, of making judgments, had begun with a seemingly innocent remark by the guide that was copied by the other group participants and had ended with everyone's feeling uncomfortable with one another.

All members of the group (and the group itself) must be accepted fully for what they are. The talk may be light and seemingly trivial; but if the guide and participants really mean what they say about acceptance, they must not pass judgment on what they think is or is not important. I have sometimes spent several hours with a group that talked about sports (or lawn care or the coming election). I did not try to move the group away from the topic, for this kind of discussion may be important. The members, or some of them, may have needed this kind of fairly inconsequential interaction in order to consolidate gains, or to feel comfortable with themselves and the others, before plunging in more deeply and moving ahead.

Here is a second example of a judgment.

> During the second meeting Vi told about her sexual dissatisfaction with her husband and said that as a consequence she sometimes masturbated. The guide, apparently trying to be accepting, said, "We all do childish things once in a while." Since when is masturbation "childish"? It is found in nearly all men and most women throughout life. But that is beside the point; to call her action childish, whatever the action might have been, was an immediate "put-down" for Vi. It was a social judgment, and neither guide nor participants were there to reinforce social censure.

When I say "Accept others for what they are," I do not mean the guide or participants must like, admire, or agree with everyone. To begin with, all group members cannot possibly have the same habits and inclinations. Too, they may not all look at convention, sex, or marriage in the same manner, due to different conditioning. But since all are at least minimally healthy and obviously like one another well enough to return for a second or third session, they can at least respond to other members as people by accepting them for what they are. We cannot remake others, but we can perhaps learn by suspending judgment and trying to empathize with their lives.

From the distorted image presented by the entertainment media, many have gotten the idea that encounter's success depends upon the number of people made to cry uncontrollably or the quantity of dramatic rage expressed. Some groups seem deliberately to encourage anger and sorrow by having group members attack one another verbally. The participants become alerted to one another's weaknesses and defenses and soon wait impatiently for their turn to probe and thrust. While such aggressiveness may be appropriate in some situations (I admittedly have my doubts), they do not belong in the kind of encounter we seek here. Our objective is to provide the nourishment of affection and encouragement, to enable growth. We supply warmth and support and in the process reduce our needs to dislike and aggress.

More will be said later about how encounter members can move away from hostility and free the feeling of love for one another as fellow human beings. The guide must know that he is responsible for making the group fully aware that attacking one another, verbally or physically, is out of bounds. The guide must protect every member and make clear that hostility, browbeating, cross-examination and abuse are not acceptable. In short, the guide functions as a protector.

The protector service of the guide is multiple. He makes certain the fundamental code of the group is maintained—no abuse, confrontation, intoxication, or other potentially harmful social behavior. He also protects members from themselves, extricating them when they seem to have gone too far and preventing them in other ways from hurting themselves. Certainly, members should not be spared any anxiety or uneasiness whatsoever. A certain amount of discomfort, even some personal suffering, is unavoidable when we examine ourselves and try to move ahead in our development. But the guide must protect members from undue anxiety lest their fears become so great that they leave the group and cease their quest for growth. The kinds of protective comments a guide (and eventually group participants themselves) might make could resemble these:

> John, you've said a great deal tonight; I feel very moved by what you said. Maybe you better pause here and give us a chance to take it all in.

> I could be wrong, Nina, but I think a few of us, certainly myself, are getting a little concerned. I wonder if it would be all right to talk about what you said so far, without going further.

In my own experience, I've found the guide has to be particularly careful that members are not picked on (even in seemingly gentle ways) by other participants. This is especially true of the quiet or withdrawn participant. Frequently people are very suspicious of those who sit demurely without saying much. Yet, as other members often find out ultimately, a lot may be happening to taciturn members as a result of their listening and sitting with the group. They often surprise others towards the end of the encounter sessions when they describe the changes that have occurred within them. Protective comments for these situations usually sound like these:

> Michael, we've talked a lot about you and what you told us this hour. It would help me if you would tell me when we've said enough. Maybe we ought to move on right now.

> I also feel that Ginny has been very quiet and not said much and frankly it makes me a little uneasy too. But I don't believe we should resent this in any way. I think we should let Ginny decide. A lot of people just take in a lot before they say very much and Ginny may be like that too.

> This last half hour I've begun to feel we may almost be picking on Calvin. Does anyone else feel that way?

The guide's protective comments teach the encounter group that people are vulnerable. They demonstrate that we need to respect each other's fragility and offer support rather than challenge. At the beginning of the encounter sessions the guide is quite likely to have to assert his protective role with some modest frequency. If he has done so effectively, and has generally become more a participant than guide, then the group members will have learned to care for one another. Towards the middle and clearly towards the end of the sessions, sufficient rapport should exist among all members that they can help themselves along, with minimal feelings of anxiety and distress.

The guide has almost a teaching function, for he will introduce techniques to help the group learn to listen and to talk.

These areas are more fully discussed in chapter 5, "Listening and Talking." In addition, like any good teacher, the guide helps the group focus on an issue or come to grips with an area when participants seem to be struggling unsteadily towards these objectives. The guide does not say, "Now let's talk about jealousy" because he thinks it is high time this is discussed. Rather, when he senses the participants have been trying to articulate this emotion for some time or feels the theme has recurred without being appropriately labeled, he might say, "I've had the feeling that what Jim and Ben, Henrietta and Gordy are talking about is jealousy." Or the guide might put it this way: "The one theme that seemed to be just beneath the surface last time, and that I think is popping out again with what we said about marriage and possessiveness, is maybe what we sometimes call jealousy."

If the guide is right the participants' faces may light up with recognition. Their interaction will have been facilitated by the revelation of the essence within a rambling discussion. If the guide is wrong this time but has honestly tried and is generally effective, the members will think no less of him for not perceiving what is being discussed on this one occasion. The guide should make it clear he is as likely to err as nearly any other group participant.

The guide may help focus discussion and on occasion even sum up what has been said, almost like an instructor. But he should not confuse his role with that of either cheerleader or psychoanalyst. The cheerleader guide comments on the group itself by saying such things as "Well we all feel pretty chipper today." Or he announces happily, "I think it's time now we all talked about Lola's problem with her boss. Let's concentrate now, gang, and see how we can all help Lola." Such group comments, even when appropriate, make members feel they are amorphous parts of some lumpy conglomerate rather than individuals. Further, such general comments make individuals uncomfortable if they do not share the guide's perception of the group, since they begin to wonder whether they are out of step. The more the guide comments on the group itself, the more he makes members uncomfortable and slows down development of individual interaction.

The psychoanalytically inclined guide has difficulty focusing discussion because he always tries to make an interpretation. *Interpretation* means telling the meaning behind what is being said. The guide who tries to interpret may say, when a participant has been talking about his difficulties with the opposite sex, "Maybe you have those problems because you have serious doubts about your own manliness." Another example of interpretation is this response to a woman who has been talking about her frustrations as an older student: "It seems to me, Debra, that the reason you are failing is because it is an unconscious way of defeating your husband's new independence. You are in effect saying that you still need him to take care of you." Little good can come from such interpretative comments. If inaccurate they are a foolish distraction. If accurate they may tear away well-established defenses prematurely, introducing considerable anxiety at an inappropriate point. Interpretations, like comments on the group itself, should be exceedingly sparse if not altogether absent. Any group or individual interpretations should be made only by highly trained and qualified encounter guides.

The good encounter guide also avoids dependency. It is very easy for group members to begin to look to the guide for impetus and direction. This is one reason I am somewhat hesitant to use certain "starter" techniques, described in chapter 4 with the appropriate cautions. By intruding too actively, the guide can very quickly find the entire weight of the encounter on his shoulders. The members wait for him to start something, turn to him to make their comment, and await his nod or glance before they talk. This is totally contrary to the purpose of the guide. If he finds himself stimulating this kind of dependency he has failed in his job. Rather than creating dependency the guide should, together with the encounter participants, evolve a norm of agreed-upon standards for the entire group.

Through what the guide does and does not do, he should be initiating a new set of behavior standards, appropriate to the particular encounter experience. In our day-to-day lives we live by norms, action guidelines, that have been largely imposed upon us. In an encounter group we have a chance to reevaluate these standards, alter them, and create new ones. The few comments and directions the guide gives at the beginning of encounter should simply point the direction in which new norms will evolve. These new norms will be both stated and unstated. For example, suggestions such as those for dress are very explicit. Less obvious and more subtle is the participants' agreement not to be hostile or judicial but instead to offer warmth and acceptance. In short, the effective guide helps the group originate a code of conduct for themselves for their encounter experience.

The guide who has helped initiate new norms, and in consequence slowly becomes less a guide than a participant, has done his job well. Much of what he accomplishes is through example. He is fully accepting, warm, and sympathetic. He does not abuse, attack, or deliberately make anyone anxious. He protects, focuses discussion, and occasionally comments, first as a guide and later more and more as a participant. At the beginning of the encounter sessions, guide comments are likely to be "structuring." These remarks are simply reiterations of the purpose and procedures for the group. For example, the guide may summarize the purpose of the encounter:

> The purpose of these sessions is to work together to help us realize our own potential.

Another guide, inclined to be wordier, might structure the purpose of the group as follows:

> These group sessions are to help us achieve something that seems to be increasingly difficult in our usual experience. We want to have deeper relationships so each of us can feel more like a valued member of a community. We can work towards that in these sessions. At the same time, as we focus on getting to know each other we will get to know ourselves and start to learn more about our own possibilities. The processes of self-actualization and group feeling are dependent upon each other and to stimulate that interaction is our goal.

At some point near the beginning the guide will also have to comment on the setting and clothing and to structure the nature of the verbal interchange. Unfortunately, because misconceptions about encounter are so widespread, he will have to include comments some participants may find unnecessary. Here's what might be said:

> We'll be meeting twice a week for two hours. We should wear simple clothing that we can feel comfortable in for sitting on the floor or moving about. It should be casual, not sexy or formal, since we want to emphasize ourselves as people rather than men or women or point out our status.
>
> In this group there will not be any nudity or embarrassing manipulations though we will sometimes touch one another. We won't be shouting at each other, or probing or abusing, but instead we'll try to help each other understand and move ahead. We need a lot of sympathy and goodwill and trust, and these are the qualities we hope to emphasize.
>
> I'll make some suggestions to get us started and we'll practice some ways to help us talk and listen.

Introductory comments such as these are repeated now and then during the early sessions. They become less and less necessary later on, for they should provide the structure for the group norm. It is even acceptable for some of these preliminary comments to be written and handed out to potential members so that they can know the kind of encounter they might experience if they join (see chapter 4). Along the same lines, this book (or something similar) could also be given out, for it will make the structure of the group quite plain. There are no "secrets" in this book, and there should not be any in any equivalent work that only the guide may know. In fact the more nearly all the members share and participate fully in the process, guiding their own encounter as soon as possible, the more likely the group will be a good one for everybody.

Chapter 4

Techniques for Starting

At the first encounter meeting the air of expectation and enthusiasm will be mingled with embarrassment, anxiety, and reluctance. Who will be first to say something, to start the complex process of establishing relationship? At this point it is often very useful to have some starter techniques available. These are icebreakers that make it easier for people to talk, overcoming their initial hesitation. But great care must be exercised in using such techniques. Starters may be appropriate to get things going during the early meetings, but they must not become substitutes for spontaneity. Whatever techniques are used should be employed very sparingly lest the group or guide unwittingly become dependent upon them.

There are no rules about when to use one or the other starter activity. But as the various activities are reviewed their particular usefulness will be pointed out. Generally all techniques should be viewed as catalysts that help bring about the objectives of encounter. In themselves they have little value, and it may not be necessary to use any of them. I also do not encourage the use of formal games. There are a number of board-type games available in which encounter participants become players. With few exceptions such games are either irrelevant or diversionary. They do not catalyze the encounter process but often result in confusion and competition. Formal games should be left out of encounter.

When techniques are used to begin the encounter they should not exceed three or four activities and should be limited to the first few meetings. By the midpoint of the encounter sessions nearly all the techniques mentioned here should have been dropped. A group still using planned activities in order to get going after four meetings probably has not developed the kind of dynamism vital for the members' growth or interaction. There are some so-called encounters which for many, many meetings are nothing but a succession of clever games, techniques, and programmed activities. Though such sessions may appeal to participants over the short term, I am very doubtful that anyone gains very much or that there are any long-term benefits.

Very often, perhaps in half of the encounters I have experienced, no starter activity is necessary. Given some introductory comments, the members are ready to go. But for those instances when some kind of icebreaker is appropriate and when due care is exercised not to impair spontaneity, some of these techniques may be employed.

Written Instructions

Structuring the meeting—that is, explaining the goals and procedures—has already been described in chapter 3, "Guiding the Group." Sometimes structuring may be accomplished by handing out a written sheet at the beginning of the first meeting. This could be a good technique if the guide wants to become a participant as soon as possible. By sharing a statement of some goals and procedures with all the members, he can prompt everyone to take an active guiding role right from the first. Here is a written description that could be used.

In order that we all understand the kind of encounter this is to be, I am giving out these typed instructions. That way we can all share in directing ourselves to common objectives.

Our goal is to get to know one another, and thereby ourselves, far better than we do in ordinary contact. Through the relationships and understandings we will experience here, we hope that all of us can move closer to realizing our own potential.

To accomplish these goals we should feel free to speak freely and without inhibition about our feelings, reactions, and thoughts. If there is any restriction it is that we should be careful to restrain our more aggressive and critical impulses. This is because one of the accompanying goals of these groups is to develop our ability to establish positive relationships with others. We want our encounter to be as free as possible of the competitiveness and hostility we frequently experience in the rest of our lives.

There are just a few simple rules that should be adhered to. Each session is two hours long and we will meet twice each week. Food and drink (especially intoxicants) are not permitted, and there should be little smoking. Participants should dress casually in a leisurely "at home" manner so that they can move about, sit on the floor, and do some of the exercises we may do later. During the duration of the encounter, members should not socialize with one another outside of the sessions.

After a handout is distributed numerous questions usually follow. These queries and statements give the guide, along with the other members, an opportunity to examine the rationale behind the written suggestions. When such opening discussions are well handled by the guide, with every member encouraged to evaluate the handout, a good interaction has begun and the group is off to a good start.

Silence

Frequently all that is needed following either a spoken or a written introduction is a short silence. The guide sits quietly, looking at everyone, and after a minute or so someone ventures forth. Because we are uneasy with silence, the quiet has acted as a very strong stimulant and members start to talk, groping for understanding and relationship. Silence—I am admittedly biased in its favor—has some very distinct advantages. First, it makes it clear to all participants that it is up to them to create a common experience. No one is going to lead them, and there are no games or activities to hide behind. Second, silence encourages reflection and deliberation. Instead of talking impulsively and compulsively, usually without much meaning, as we do in so much of our ordinary lives, we are prompted to explore ourselves unhurriedly. When we take the time to pause and reflect, we can become aware as never before of both ourselves and others and of our mutual interaction.

Combining a nice structuring statement (written or spoken) with silence frequently leads to excellent comments and innovations. Here are some statements made by participants at the beginning of a first meeting, demonstrating the variety of thoughts often produced.

> Discussion starts as to whether one gets rid of aggression by holding it in or letting it out—should we restrain aggressive comments or is it healthier to get feelings off our chest.

> Participants question whether group should meet for long or short periods, indoors or outdoors, and consider rationale behind suggestion of two-hour meetings.

> Group decides to have each member in turn recite a poem or make a short topical speech in order to warm up.

> Participants begin to consider whether there should be just one guide or whether members should rotate responsibility for reminding the group of procedures and targets. Eventually an excellent rotating guide system is worked out and carried through.

> In response to a participant's question, all take turns discussing their motives for coming.

> Group decides to make up names for one another. There is vigorous discussion about why certain people should or should not be called Bob or Chuck or Stretch or Rose, etc.

Group decides to begin communication by writing to one another anonymous notes.

Occasionally a group has trouble using silence as a way of initiating the encounter. After the guide has structured, most encounter members feel an awkward sense of aloneness. They are usually highly self-conscious, and it takes a little daring to make the first remark. In those infrequent situations in which no one starts, the members may begin to resent their situation. They feel the guide has taken two or three minutes to explain the purpose and then cast everyone adrift. Consequently, now and again a group will react to silence by turning to the guide and trying to persuade and cajole him to get things started. Sometimes members can even be quite critical, implying the guide is not doing his job, does not want to help, or is using them as part of some unethical psychological experiment. But this is not a serious disadvantage of silence, and such initial anxiety and suspicion is usually overcome by reassurance and patience.

Silence is a valuable technique, not only at the beginning but also within sessions. Sooner or later, regardless of whether the encounter was begun using silence, members will have to accustom themselves to sitting quietly and thinking. Every minute of every encounter does not have to be filled with talk. If the guide has used an approach other than silence as a starter, he will have to introduce this approach at appropriate moments later in the encounter. The group should be made aware, probably fairly early, that the guide is not there to jump in with some game, technique, or question whenever no one else speaks. Periods of silence are important and may be as much a communication as words.

Introductions

An easy and natural starter technique, because it is what we often do on our own, is to ask all members to introduce themselves. Participants are instructed to give their names, tell their marital or family status, describe their work and interests, and say a few words about their expectations for this group. Each person takes a turn introducing himself.

Formative Happening

In this starter technique, members are asked (in turn or spontaneously) to describe the two or three events or circumstances in their lives that helped make them what they are now. The experience related can be negative or positive. Here is an example of such a description; the narrator is a 20-year-old woman.

> I got very hurt by an older friend of mine when I was seventeen. Nothing she did to me in particular. I had gone through a very bad period with her. She was in the process of getting a divorce and she was having an affair and she felt absolutely miserable about it and she was seeing a psychiatrist. It was really heavy, a heavy period for her. She'd come over to my house and cry. I went through this with her. I would hold her and let her cry and try to comfort her. And then it was over, she got her divorce and her boyfriend and there was nothing anymore for me.
>
> I was no more use to her and I began to feel really bad. I'd try to talk about it with her and she just put up a wall. She'd say she couldn't understand or that she didn't want to deal with this. And I took it personally. And was very hurt by it. Which I shouldn't have taken personally, I see now.
>
> There was a period about a year and a half when I kinda withdrew from everybody, from all of my friends. I wanted to sort things out, why I felt so low and bad. Trying to look at things clearly. Being more objective. I've never been a very objective person. I lead with my emotions rather than with my head and that period was a drawing back. I'm very glad I went through it although it was an extremely painful period at the time. Because I need contact with people and to force myself to do without that was painful.

Who Am I

In this technique members are instructed to tell as much as they can about themselves using only five words. Individuals and groups will differ considerably in how they interpret this instruction. Some will give such relatively objective information as this:

> Father, accountant, Dartmouth alumnus, Catholic, tennis player.
> Woman, dancer, tall, college dropout, agnostic.

Some members may talk about their personality or ambitions and say things like these:

> Shy, fearful, easily worried, up-tight, sad.
> Curious, tense, sexy, persistent, aggressive.
> Religious, stubborn, intelligent, ambitious, stingy.

Often a first round of "Who Am I" is fairly quick and not very productive. It is worthwhile to try a second and third round. Typically by the time participants have said ten to fifteen descriptive words about themselves they are beginning to know one another and respond to the cues offered by another person's self-description.

Parent Description

In this technique the participants are asked to describe both mother and father in some detail. Frequently this is an excellent opener, for it may involve as much self-description as parent description. At times, also, members show considerable emotion in telling about their father or mother, to which other members often respond warmly.

First Impression

This activity requires each participant to give his first impression of everyone else. Usually I qualify this by suggesting that a positive first impression be given. This is a good way to encourage a positive outlook and make members less self-conscious. Everyone will have some positive things said about him and consequently feel a little closer to the other people who were once total strangers. Here are some typical comments:

I liked the way you walked in. I thought there was a man with purpose in his stride.

I thought the way you sat, so casual, looked like you were just a nice and relaxed guy.

When I looked around the room and saw you were smiling I figured that you were very kind. You were trying to make me feel better.

I noticed the shape of your hands. I thought they were expressive and creative hands. You seemed like a very talented person, even the way you dressed.

Predictions

Participants discuss what they would like to be and do five to ten years hence and what they believe their situation will actually be. Often this leads to discussion about why some believe they will or will not accomplish their objectives.

Intimate Questions

In this activity members of the group are given pencil and paper and asked to write the one or two most intimate questions they could be asked. They are told that the questions will be collected, randomly distributed to assure anonymity, and then read aloud by the person who is assigned that question. This person will then have to play a part, to discuss and respond as if he had written that question himself—that is, he is not to answer truthfully; he is to make up a role, to act an answer. Here are some frequently written questions:

If you could change your life, how would you change it?
Have you ever tried to commit suicide?
What have you done that you are very ashamed of?
Have you ever really loved anyone?
Have you ever been attracted by the same sex?
Have you ever wanted to really hurt anyone else?
Are you too aware of yourself physically?
What are you most afraid of?

Do you love yourself?
Why did you and your husband separate?

Closed Eyes

After the participants have been given a chance to introduce themselves, giving little more than their names, they are
requested to close their eyes or are blindfolded. They then
begin a discussion in which no one knows who is talking or
responding. These in-the-dark, anonymous interactions can
quickly develop considerable depth. In order to get a closed-
eye group talking for about an hour, one of the other discus-
sion-stimulating techniques may be tried or members may
simply be asked if anyone wants to say anything.

Values

Group members are asked to imagine they have the knowl-
edge, foresight, and funds necessary to secretly build a space-
ship:

> Within a few weeks the final all-out nuclear war will totally
> destroy Earth. You will guide your ship to a newly discovered
> uninhabited planet that is hospitable to human life and is one
> year's travel away. Your ship has food and room for only five
> others. Who will you save? Who will you take with you to the
> new world and perhaps start human life and culture all over
> again?

This "Noah's Ark" activity can lead to very lively and prob-
ing discussion. Very early, right at the beginning of encounter,
members are being forced to examine their beliefs and values
quite critically as they are asked why they pick one person or
leave another. Here is an excerpt from a spirited discussion:

Al: I would just take my wife and my three children. Then to
   make five I would take a doctor along. He could be very
   helpful.
Sue: Why did you say "he," right away? Couldn't the doctor
   be a woman?

Al: All right. I have no objection. In fact I would take a woman doctor, and she would have to be young and pretty. (*Everyone laughs and Sue seems displeased.*) I mean it. I want two women. My wife and the doctor and I would share and share alike.

Henry: There is a lot you have left out, Al. There are a lot of different races and religions in the world. You wouldn't be taking any of them.

Willy: Aren't you just being goody-goody taking just your family?

Al: No. No I am not being just a goody. I think my children are really great. They're intelligent, kind and loving and that's what I want the new world to be. My wife and I have grown together and we are closer to each other than any couple I know. We need each other and I would need her.

Sam: If you're so perfect what are you doing in this group?

Milly: That may not be entirely fair. Al might have a very good family and still want more from himself.

Al: Thanks, Milly, I think that we all want more. I have it good at home and I am very happy about it. That's why I don't feel it necessary to save the world and take someone from this group or that.

Lynn: I think we know where Al is at. Let me tell you what I've been thinking. I don't really know for sure this is what I would do but it occurred to me that I would take only five very young children. I would want to raise them just the way I want. There would be nothing else but me. You know, no television, movies, or neighbors or school system or anything. I would raise them just the way they should be.

My Bias

In this activity members are asked to explain their stand on some controversial issue. They are not to give the usual rational arguments for or against a point of view but instead to tell why they personally support one side or another. Why are they biased in one direction? Areas are suggested by the guide, as a starter, and then other participants introduce topics. Typical issues are abortion, racial and ethnic equality, fidelity in marriage, capital punishment, free enterprise, socialism, and religious beliefs. Here a young woman discusses marital fidelity:

> The reason I am biased for marital fidelity is that I was raised that way. I grew up in a Christian home and that was the way you were supposed to do things. It was just wrong, morally wrong, to be unfaithful. I remember how my mother would sneer at one family where the man had a reputation for that sort of thing. I just grew up believing, deep down in my bones, that it was wrong.

(*Another group member: But why do you hang on to that belief? You sound like you don't still believe it just because you were taught to believe it.*)

> Well I guess that is true. I don't believe lots of things anymore my parents taught me. I guess I still believe this because I want to or maybe I need to. Maybe it's that I am scared to believe anything else. I guess that if I said to my husband I didn't believe in fidelity then I would lose him. I suppose that's why I say I believe in the absolutely faithful marriage so much. I know Jim would not leave me but I am afraid he might find another woman more attractive than me. I guess you could say I believe in fidelity because I am scared.

Notice in this example that the interaction, even this early in encounter, led to a very worthwhile insight for the young wife. She was able to trace at least one of the reasons why she felt strongly about fidelity. A personalized discussion of prejudices about a controversial issue can start some very good interactions and self-understanding.

Singing

Some encounter professionals suggest the participants shout, yell, cry, or make noise to unwind, relax, and ready themselves to pour out their feelings. I am somewhat doubtful about the value of such exaggerated vocal pyrotechnics, though some members report this makes them feel good. Some groups sing, and this might be worth trying with a group that would find more demanding starter techniques less acceptable. Encounters with older or retired members have sometimes been started in this way, apparently with success. Another kind of group that has been reported to respond positively to singing is at the other end of the age scale—teenagers involved in a church-sponsored encounter.

Tape Recorder

Sound or video taping of encounters has become very popular. Meetings are recorded and then played back to let members see and/or hear their participation. Sometimes this is useful in discussing self-images. Someone may mistakenly think he is weak or self-effacing or have some other belief about himself which a recording can dramatically contradict. One fairly aggressive and domineering member could not believe that he monopolized the encounter and was overly critical of others. But when he saw a videotape of himself, he was easily convinced. Similarly a female participant believed she was graceless, mousy-looking, and overly anxious until she saw herself on videotape. There was no doubt about the charm of her bearing and the genteelness of her manner; a whole new self-image was initiated by the experience.

These may be very worthwhile uses of recording devices, but I believe they do not really belong in an encounter setting. I know that taping early comments and replaying them in various ways can stimulate some insight and interaction. But I believe the purpose of encounter is ultimately subverted by introducing technology which can seriously impair spontaneity. If what a member does now is going to be reviewed, his current activity can easily become a play-acted projection for later use. Thus while I might concur with a minimal amount of tape recording at the very beginning, just as an ice-breaker, I feel such devices should best not be used at all. Incidentally, many psychologists (myself included) do record encounter sessions, with the permission of all members. This is simply a way to help them recollect events (if they work with several groups) or to make use of the discussion for research, writing, or training. Such a recording is not played back to the members, and it is of course treated with the strictest confidentiality.

Sensitivity Techniques

Just as I do not recommend recording devices, I do not recommend many of the so-called sensitivity techniques such as "trust" walks. In a trust walk one member is blindfolded and led around by another, thereby supposedly developing trust. Other sensitivity exercises require a member to study the palm of his hand, pull apart a flower, or sit in the rain so that he may become more aware of the ordinary, which we too often take for granted. There is value in such activities— they may heighten awareness—but I do not believe they contribute much to human encounter. Like tape recorders and other machinery, they may in fact detract from the primary purpose, which is to stimulate person-to-person interaction.

Wise and Foolish

A good way to start encounter with many groups is to ask each member to describe the stupidest, dumbest, or most foolish thing he or she has ever done. After this activity has gone the rounds, in order to close on a more positive note members are asked to talk about the smartest, wisest thing they have ever done. Stories similar to these are likely to be heard:

> The dumbest thing I ever did was to get myself in trouble with the police. When I was away at school I was getting very low on money. I had developed some expensive habits. I mean it was not that I needed the money for food or books. I needed it for clothes, tapes, my car, you know, and having a good time. Well to make a long story short, I began to steal. I would take anything that wasn't tied down. Books, speakers, radios, watches, bikes and whatever I could sell in town. I got to know some pretty shady characters that would buy the stuff from me. Well I got caught red handed and I got thrown out of school and the whole business. I went to

court and they let me plead guilty to a misdemeanor so I got off with a suspended sentence. But I got a record and that doesn't do you any good.

I think the smartest thing I ever did was when I left home. Ever since then I have known I can make it on my own. My mother was so protective and domineering and she made me feel so dumb. When I left I was convinced I was going to collapse but I made it. It was never easy, in fact it was agony, believe me. But when I made it then I knew I could always depend upon myself and could make it anywhere. That decision, to be on my own, was the smartest thing I ever did.

The Work of Encounter

Encounter is hard work. There is a temptation to let the techniques or guide, or on one especially vocal group mem-decide what to say and do next. But the tendency to rely on techniques or guide, or on one especially vocal group member, must be diligently resisted. All participants must learn to contribute and put forth an earnest effort. Some have the impression that encounter is no more than an entertainment: all that needs to be done is to sit back and let things happen. When such entertainment attitudes prevail very little will come of the sessions. But when all participants vigorously pursue their common purpose and are willing to endure some anxiety and discomfort, they will often feel satisfyingly fatigued, both psychologically and physically, at the end of a session. Meaningful encounter can leave one exhausted but also exhilarated with new thoughts and feelings.

Chapter 5

Listening and Talking

The purpose of encounter is to increase self-awareness and deepen interaction with others. To reach these related goals participants talk about their feelings and aspirations. They describe themselves as they are now, try to uncover how they became that way, and slowly develop new potentials within themselves. All this takes place in a group setting with members talking to and assisting one another.

In some ways such discussions do not differ from ordinary conversations between friends and acquaintances. Certainly the primary topic members discuss, themselves, is something we all dwell on whether in psychotherapy, encounter, or casual talk with an acquaintance. What distinguishes an encounter conversation from the ordinary is the radically different way people listen and respond. People cannot simply transfer their day-to-day conversational habits to an encounter and expect a deepening of feeling, understanding, or growth. In encounter people must substantially change the way they listen and respond.

57

Listening

Few of us really listen to others or even expect to be listened to. We know that what we relate is only half heard because we ourselves have only fractional interest in the stories of others. While they talk we are busy thinking about our own similar experience or waiting impatiently to interrupt with a critical comment or question. Most conversations, as a result, are simply parallel talk. Several people discuss a generally similar topic with little or no direct reaction to one another. Here is a representative excerpt from a conversation at a dinner party:

Bernie: I had to go home to take my mother to the hospital. She is getting very old and she didn't really understand what was going on. Some weekend, last week.

Hilda: My mother is 52 and she looks 40. She doesn't age.

Nick: You still seem kind of set back by it, Bernie.

Bill: I can't remember when I saw my parents last. Christmas I think. I don't really know.

Hilda: My mother doesn't like Christmas. She's always got the blues that time of year.

Nick: Is your mother very sick, Bernie?

Bernie: She may not make it. The doctor said it was probably a blood clot. They couldn't tell.

Leslie: My older brother had a blood clot or something and they operated on his chest. He's still paying the bill. His hospital insurance was worthless. I told him then, he called up long distance, just when we were getting ready for our vacation, and he was going to the hospital. . . .

Hilda: We never take a vacation. The most we'll be able to get away is a long weekend.

Bernie: I was never that close to my mother but you feel a responsibility. I thought maybe. . . .

Hilda: My mother is a pill. I mean it may not be nice to say but she can be so crabby. . . .

Leslie: Well, let me tell you, here we were getting ready to go

off, and my brother calls. I mean, I was furious. I mean, he's a big boy now. . . .
Nick: How's your mother doing now, Bernie?

In this conversation it looks very much as if the only one at least listening to Bernie to some degree is Nick. He seems genuinely concerned about Bernie and his mother. The others have no interest in either Bernie or anyone else; they are simply intent on telling their own stories. During encounter members have to alter these conversational habits drastically. Instead of focusing on irrelevant details or concentrating on their own stories and reactions they need to listen fully and intentionally. They want to really hear what the other person is saying. This does not mean, however, that they sit silently. Listening is an active process. If we simply stare dumbly at someone talking he will soon cease. Listening requires us to respond, to talk, and in encounter the talk will be mainly agreement, restatement, and reflection. Reflection will be discussed in chapter 6, "Reflecting Feeling," while agreement and restatement will be detailed here.

Agreeing

Much everyday discussion is simply parallel talk. But when we do listen, we conventionally demonstrate our interest mainly by being critical and only secondarily by being supportive. We question, dispute, argue, and rarely agree. During encounter members have to reverse this order. Their responses to those who speak must be primarily supportive and minimally, very minimally, critical. In order to listen completely and not interfere with the other person's expression, they must strain to hear and not strain to think of clever critical comments.

Here is another conversation from the same dinner party mentioned before. To help the reader notice all the critical comments, questions, contradictions, and attacks, I have labeled some of them.

Bill: How are things going, Nick?

Nick: So-so. I can't seem to get a raise from my boss. I may even be fired.

Bill: How come? Why does he want to fire you?

Nick: Well it's not that he wants to fire me as much as it is that I'm sick and tired of that work.

Bill: You don't have a bad job. Why would you say you're sick and tired of it? (*This is a criticism of Nick's feelings and judgment.*)

Nick: The boss is an S.O.B. You can't please him.

Bill: You've got to learn to get along with S.O.B.'s (*Another criticism.*)

Nick: Nobody could get along with him. He's impossible.

Bill: Don't say that, he's got his problems just like everyone else. You could get along with him if you wanted. (*Contradiction.*)

Nick: If he gave me a raise I would be better off.

Bill: Since when have you become an agitator? (*Another critical question.*)

Nick: I'm only asking for my rights.

Bill: Yeah, and he's got his rights too.

Nick: I'm really feeling lousy nowadays.

Bill: No kidding, how come?

Is it any wonder that Nick is "feeling lousy nowadays," with friends like Bill? After continually disputing with, contradicting, and criticizing Nick, Bill is extremely unlikely to really understand him or his situation. If Bill had been supportive, had indicated his genuine interest and concern, Bill would have had an opportunity not only to advise his friend but to probe his own feelings more extensively.

Contrast the preceding dialogue with a conversation about a fairly similar topic in an encounter in which everyone listened intently and indicated rapport through agreement.

June: I felt so good all weekend until I had to go back to work on Monday.

(*Several group members nod understandingly. June continues.*)

June: My work is just so frustratingly routine. On weekends I become a person. Then it all comes crashing down around my ears on Mondays.

(*Several group members nod agreement or say "Hm mm."*)

June: Everything is just so old by now. They always have the same old jokes, and you know what everyone will wear and you're going to get the same assignments. I feel like if this is going to be the way it is maybe I ought to gather up my courage and quit.

Mel: Uh huh.

June: That's right. I refuse to put up with being half a person for five days and just waiting breathlessly for the weekend.

(*No one comments but several members nod understandingly to June or say "Hm mm."*)

June: I thought I might go back to school. I might become something else. But then I get discouraged about that too because that could be a terrific burden at my stage of life. I'm used to making money and it's brought me a lot of luxuries. I just don't know where to turn.

Mel: Uh huh, you don't know where to turn.

June: That's exactly how I feel. I'm depressed. I'm scared too. But, really maybe, I know what I'm going to do. I might just quit. Maybe I could live with being scared and maybe even depressed for a while, so I can do something new. You have to pay a price for something new and good.

In this brief interchange, with the group doing little more than indicating agreement, June was able to work through to an understanding on her own. She began by complaining and ended by seeing a new direction for her life. When comments are critical (my term for questioning, disputing, attacking) they are very unlikely to help the conversational partner advance. But when they are supportive (agreeing, restating, reflecting) they help the person reach further within himself and develop his own potential.

Agreement, the first of the supportive talk techniques, is indicated by an affirmative nod of the head, saying "Hm mm" or "Uh huh," or by any equivalent vocalization or behavior. These agreement responses are a way of signaling the speaker that we are listening, understand, and want him to continue. We are not necessarily indicating that what he describes is absolutely correct. We are not agreeing that "yes, your husband *is* a miserable wretch." We are agreeing rather that "yes, as you describe it, I can understand that you feel your husband is a miserable wretch." Agreement means that we are entering the thinking and emotional life of the person talking so thoroughly that we are beginning to experience the world almost as that person does.

It may be objected that agreement just helps others confirm their own opinions. Should not another's prejudices be attacked in order to show him the error of his biases? Critical attack may win an occasional debate. In most human interactions, however, disagreement (not agreement) rigidifies thought. When we tell someone he is wrong he immediately mobilizes every argument and defense to prove himself right. But if we nod understandingly we are far more likely to help the other evaluate himself and perhaps rethink some of his conclusions.

Encounter members might try agreement as an exercise, outside the group, to demonstrate to themselves how often it leads to surprising insight and modification. What happens if we talk to someone very bigoted and nod understandingly as he trots out his biases? By agreement we encourage him to go on, and before too long our positive understanding may result in his toning down his original prejudices. Here is an example of such a conversation with a fellow worker, reported by an encounter participant. (The name of the ethnic group is omitted, and "Blank" is substituted.)

Bigot: The Blanks want to take over. They've got their secret army and everything. They got the guns; you read about it all the time.

Encounter Member: Hm mm.

Bigot: You bet, they're the ones that commit all the crimes. They're out to rob the country.

E.M.: They're robbing the country.

Bigot: That's the way I see it. With them around nobody is safe. You can't walk the streets and at night you better stay home. I don't care whether it's a good neighborhood or bad, nobody is safe anymore.

E.M.: They're the ones that make the neighborhoods unsafe.

Bigot: No, I'm not saying that they're the only ones that do it. I mean you read about lots of other people committing crimes and all, but they do a lot.

E.M.: So most of the crime is what they do.

Bigot: I don't know if you would say most or a lot. But they do a lot. I mean especially the crime where they attack you. I mean I know the bigshots do the big stuff, I mean you only see a little of what they're up to in the paper now and then. But the Blanks, they do the kind of stuff that makes you and me afraid to take a walk at night.

E.M.: So we have to be afraid of the Blanks because they threaten us physically.

Bigot: That's right, they threaten us physically. But the big-timers, they're the ones that's taking it from us all the time.

The conversation continued, and this relatively bigoted individual, by being encouraged to go on in his description and thinking, eventually perceived the Blank ethnic group in a new light. He may not have become unbiased overnight simply by being allowed to talk, but he was well beyond where he might have been if critical responses had forced him to muster arguments and opinions to solidify his position.

The following conversation is from an early encounter and nicely illustrates appropriate agreement responses. To demonstrate how persons might talk in everyday interaction I played a tape of this conversation to non-encounter people, asking them to indicate their reactions. In parentheses are the resultant everyday comments that should *not* be made.

Lou: I really began to know myself about four years ago, around this time it started. I was living in the city and I was pretty isolated. . . .

(Everyday comments: Why didn't you get out more? Where were you living?)

(*Encounter group members say nothing. Several nod their heads and say "Hm mm."*)

Lou: I was taking a lot of trips. All sorts of messed up junk and stuff, that I could get a hold of.

(Everyday: What kind of drugs were you taking? Why were you doing that? Don't you think you would have been better off not taking drugs?)

(*Group simply indicates agreement.*)

Lou: I had my own apartment and I was working and really out of contact with people. And even the type of work I was doing, I would deliver things, and then I'd go home.

(Everyday: Delivering what? What were they paying you? Didn't you work with people you could talk with? Where was your apartment?)

Lou: So anyway, this one Sunday I said God, I have to get out of this, you know. I just felt like it was a death trap. I felt I was just wasting away. . . . So anyway, I was looking through the paper and I saw this school job up in the country and at that point I was like stuck you know, into a real grind, there was no way out of it. . . .

(Everyday: You seem smart enough to get a better job. You must be very religious or else superstitious. Did you feel like suicide?)

Encounter Member: You felt stuck, like there was no way out. . . .

Lou: Right, I was doing a whole lot of things the wrong way and the only way I could get out of it was by getting away from that whole situation. . . . So I called up this school in the country and got a nine-dollar phone bill, which was kind of weird, and three days afterward I sold out my apartment and packed my stuff and went up there and it was unbelievable in terms of the change that I was getting myself to go into.

(Everyday: Are you a religious person, Lou, I mean since it all came to you on a Sunday? Do you think you can really change just by changing jobs or your apartment? Why didn't you go to a drug clinic and get some medical help? It was irresponsible to run up such a big phone bill.)

(*Encounter members register sympathetic understanding and several nod their heads or say "Hm mm."*)

Lou: I met a girl up there and I got involved with her and I got involved with a lot of people. Like I wouldn't say it was night and day but it was really a new life for me. And because of that I stopped taking all the drugs I was taking, and the tranquilizers. . . . They were all just killing me. I was sort of a counselor for these retarded kids and I really had to be in good shape to help them. Like they really needed me, they depended upon me.

(*Encounter members indicate agreement, several smile warmly.*)

(Everyday: How retarded were these kids? Was it a private school? Do you have a college degree? Don't you think you should have told the school about your drug abuse? What were the people like up there?)

Lou: So in about two months I had really transformed myself. I started getting involved with other people and changing my whole approach to life. I started seeing I was worth something to some people.

The everyday comments are from non-encounter men and women told only that when the tape stopped they were to react as if they were personally conversing with Lou. If Lou had actually been questioned critically and commented upon by the tape listeners, he would never have reached the point he was trying to make, to show how his entire personality changed. Thus the first requirement of encounter dialogue is for all members to indicate their silent and spoken agreement, in order to let the person tell what he has to tell, fully and completely and in his own way.

Restatement

In encounter sessions agreement is usually indicated by a simple nod, an "Uh huh," a warm smile, or similar indication that "I understand what you are saying." But at times these direct and clear indications may not be enough. The person talking may want more complete reassurance that others understand, or he may have wandered so far in his description that he actually depends upon others to help redirect him. In these and similar instances members can indicate agreement by restating, in a sense summarizing, what has been said. Their comment might sound like this:

> As I understand what you are saying, Nancy, it's that you were working under the idea that your sister actually wanted you to be better, so she could complain to your parents and get you in trouble.

Restatement is not easy. Unlike agreement, which is conveyed by "Hm mm" or the like, restatements can be long and complex. Members must concentrate with every faculty on what is being said to summarize accurately. And, as never before, they need to guard against any tendency to think of clever questions and rebuttals. Here is an excerpt from an encounter dialogue that contains several important restatements.

Giselle: I told him we were through. I didn't want to live with him or see him or have anything more to do with him. He made me feel weak and stupid and if that was his game I was not going to play it. After three months I think it wasn't unreasonable of me to put it to him. I want to start off in a new direction.

Mindy: He made you feel incompetent and you think you will be better off without him.

Giselle: Yes, and my mother was giving me hell whenever we

came. She wouldn't let him in. She called him my paramour. And Janey, my oldest, didn't like him at all. I wonder why I put up with it so long. Next time, if there is a next time, I'm going to watch out for myself first of all, I'm not going to let sympathy or pity take over. . . . I don't know, I just don't know if I am right.

Derek: The way I understand it, Giselle, and maybe I'm confused, is that there were a lot of bad things about your relationship but you are still not sure you were right.

Giselle: You're right. I could go on and tell you all the lousy things between us and everything. But still and all I don't know if maybe I didn't get more out of it than I thought I was. You can't tell sometimes till it's over.

Derek: Uh huh.

Giselle: Well here it is as I see it. I want him and I don't want him. He's good for me as a woman, but not as a mother or a person in my own right. If I want to be more than a woman I can't put up with him. So maybe that's it. If I want to become more than I have been I can't let him and his attitudes stand in the way.

Mindy: So what you are saying is that if you want to develop your own potential more, he's in the way. At least that's how you seem to be seeing it now, as I get it.

Giselle: That's right. Hm mm. I need to go on past him.

Accurate restatement is a challenge, and some encounter participants may question if they have the ability to understand and summarize what another says. After all, some participants may argue, they are not psychologists and cannot be expected to remember all that another discusses. What if they make a mistake and summarize erroneously?

These are legitimate questions and fears, but such doubts need not be disabling. First of all, in encounter members are not playing games or tricks with one another. They are not competing to see who can make the best or cleverest restatement. They are restating both to help themselves know whether they understand and to prompt and encourage the one talking. Further, if someone does make a restatement that is erroneous, no harm is done. The person talking has a chance to correct the misunderstanding so that both can go ahead together. Missing the point when restating is not a weakness; it is a strength, because it provides a new opportunity to invigorate rapport.

Walter: I wanted to go with him. He wanted me to stay because I would miss too much time on my job. But I kept telling him that he meant a lot to me, too much to let him go that far without being with him. It was just one of those kinds of companionships. We were comrades, you might say, and I wanted to continue. But he was concerned about how it would look. That's why I think he wanted to cool our relationship. But he just couldn't come right out and say it, he wanted to make it easy.

Tim: He didn't want you along because he didn't like you like that anymore.

Walter: No, he liked me all right. He didn't like what it looked like on the outside. You know, he was afraid of appearances so he thought it would look better if we were separated for a while. I mean he really liked me all right. He said it to me very clearly, and that I believe. I mean, you know, I was also worried about what it looked like but I thought there could be a better way to make it look all right than just leaving alone.

Here is another example of a "miss" in restatement. Yet obviously, with correction the speakers have moved even closer together.

Jan: I told my sister I would not pay for it. It simply wasn't my responsibility. It was her business. If she wanted to spend her share of the bequest by paying for the cottage she could do it. So she told me she was older and she knew more about these things and it was a good investment. So we were right back to where we were when she was always taking charge of me and she knew better. I mean that is why I did not want to buy it for any reason. I was not about to let her boss me again and it was time she knew it. Then my aunt wrote and said it was really all broken down and was a real bargain. So I thought maybe it would be a good investment after all. But I did not want her interference again since it's about the third time this happened this year and I have had it.

Dennis: You just didn't want to be bossed around by your older sister, is that right?

Jan: No, I don't think so. Is that what I said?

Dennis: I think so. That's how I understood it.

Jessie: Yes, I think I understood it that way too. But could you have been saying you changed your mind, that maybe you would buy because it was a good investment and never mind how you felt about your sister.

Jan: I think that's what I wanted to say, Dennis. Like Jessie says, I think I gave you that impression because I'm very confused myself. I mean you have been following my thoughts quite well, I mean you really seem to understand what I am saying, but I don't always work it out so well. I think maybe we seem to understand each other usually because you've got a lot of questions that are like mine. I mean at least I think I have noticed that.

Jessie: Hm mm, I think I've seen that.

Dennis: Well I couldn't quite follow you before, but I do agree we come from very similar backgrounds so very often I follow what you say very easily.

Exercises

There is no magic in "Hm mm" or restatement. These are simply affirmative ways to listen and respond. They provide the speaker with the interest and concern he needs to continue and prompt him to go on, reaching further and further into his thoughts and emotions. Sometimes participants may want to try a few exercises, within or outside encounter, to sharpen their abilities to listen, agree, and restate. Here are some suggestions:

1. *Listen.* Participants spend a day just listening to everyone they talk to. They do no more than just nod agreement, say "Hm mm," smile appreciatively, or the equivalent. They notice that most people are unused to being listened to. At first people may pause several times, expecting to be interrupted. But eventually they will continue, feeling encouraged to talk as they seldom have felt before.

2. *Critical-Supportive Roles.* Participants may want to spend a part of their session playing alternately critical and supportive roles with each other. Two members volunteer to play each role in turn in discussing a controversial and topical issue, while the rest listen to see the difference in interaction. Here Sue and Tony have decided to talk first about permissiveness, playing critical roles, and then about birth control, playing supportive roles.

Sue: I think we're much too permissive with kids today. We let them do whatever they want in school or at home or anywhere. . . .

Tony: Oh no, we're not. Kids need freedom to grow. You were probably raised very strict, that's why you say that.

Sue: No, that's not true. I had good parents that cared about me but they didn't let me run loose all over. I think children want to have some guidelines.

Tony: I read that this psychiatrist said most parents were too strict. Kids have just as much ability as grownups to make up their own mind.

Sue: I don't think so. You can't believe everything you read about what some psychiatrist said.

Tony: I saw it in one of those parents' magazines, what they tell you is the way it is, not the way some up-tight parents think it is.

Sue: Well I'm not up-tight and those magazines print a lot of garbage.

Tony: So now you know more than a psychiatrist.
Sue: I am not saying I know more, I'm just saying that what I know is different from what you know.

When such critical conversations are role-played, encounter participants very quickly recognize how often their own social interaction follows similar patterns and how easily such conversation becomes acrimonious debate. In vivid contrast, here are the same participants role-playing support.

Tony: The only way you're going to solve the population problem is for all the world's governments to agree to limit all parents to only two children.
Sue: Hm mm.
Tony: You just can't let people go on indefinitely having five or six children. Our resources are limited and we just have to cut down our family size.
Sue: You feel we are running out of resources and we have to limit the population.
Tony: Uh huh, and we can only do it if the government makes it mandatory. People won't do it on their own voluntarily.
Sué: The government would have to prohibit more than two children.
Tony: Right, they could do it like by giving you a payment for every child you did not have or something, or requiring you to get a license to have a child and then only issue two licenses to you and like that. We might not have to do it forever. Maybe just for one or two generations till our food supplies and technology catch up.
Sue: So you feel this might be like a temporary way to halt the population explosion.
Tony: Yes, and since the burden would fall on everybody equally it wouldn't be unfair.

The difference between this supportive role-playing and the preceding critical one is like that between night and day. No matter which side of a controversy we endorse, supportive interaction permits us to learn about another's viewpoint. Critical conversation, on the other hand, does nothing but bring accusations, ill will, anger, and frustration. If members want to help each other in encounter they must learn to make their interaction supportive. There is a place for questioning and contradicting, in a very limited way (chapter 7, "Questions, Contradictions, and Anger"), but primary interchange must consist of agreement, restatement, and occasionally reflection (discussed in the following chapter).

Chapter 6

Reflecting Feelings

The mechanics of encounter are words, but the dynamics are feelings. We use words to describe ourselves, our reactions, and our ambitions. But underlying our talk are changes taking place in motives, feelings, and ultimately behavior. One of the most effective verbal mechanisms we ourselves may use to help others change is reflection. This technique, like restatement, consists essentially of underlining the feelings being expressed by another. We listen carefully and whenever appropriate make a comment like "You seem to feel angry," or "That frightened you."

Why underline, point out, or focus on feeling? The answer lies in the view of personality and human potential suggested by such psychologists as Carl Rogers and Abraham Maslow. They see humans as fundamentally sound and positive. But no sooner is the child born than punitive parents, challenging peers, and a repressive society begin to distort and disable every good motive, aspiration, and feeling. The child begins

to suspect and dislike his own physiological drives; he re-
presses affectional needs, and instead of actualizing his potential he becomes narrowed, inhibited, and inadequate. In short,
he builds up a massive defensive armor of punitive and anxious
emotions about himself, others, and the world.

But while the individual is being rigidified by negative feelings he experiences the ever-present positive, drive to emerge
and grow. Just as our physical self experiences growth and
healing, our psychological self seeks to evolve and repair. In
psychoanalysis self-growth may be accomplished by vigorous
dissection of defensive obstacles and exploration of new alter-
natives. In the Rogers variety of psychotherapy, called *client-
centered,** the growth forces are mobilized and negative forces
relieved by pointing them out. Client-centered therapists have
found that one of the surest ways to assist their patients to
overcome negative feelings (and simultaneously allow positive ones to emerge) is to reflect the emotions of their clients.

In the typical client-centered treatment situation, massive
amounts of negative feeling are revealed at first. The client
talks about bitter emotions towards himself, his relatives, and
his friends. He is likely to see his whole existential world in
negative tones. There is hate, anger, frustration, loneliness,
inferiority, jealousy, and every other sad and disabling feeling
imaginable. But then slowly, as the therapist assists by reflecting, positive emotions begin to emerge. Tentatively at first, but
then with increasing momentum as the months go by, enthusiasm, affection, and all sorts of beneficent feelings emerge.
Rogers himself says that when an appropriate milieu is pro-
vided and a meaningful and helpful relationship established,
evolution from negative to positive feelings is a certain and
predictable outcome. The old negative feelings are both obstacles and defenses which, as they are removed, allow for the
emergence of new and life-enhancing emotions.

Client-centered therapy is so named because patients take the
lead in determining the direction of treatment. The therapist does not
push, prod, or direct his client but helps him discover his own path
and potential.

I have been discussing individual psychotherapy here, but encounter is not psychiatric treatment. Members do not come together to heal serious psychological maladaptations. Nevertheless they can use the insights and revelations of psychotherapy to help them build a worthwhile interaction. We can paraphrase the words of Rogers, written for therapy, into an encounter context:

> With proper care we can reflect in encounter and help others rid themselves of their handicapped feelings. We can help expose that which is disabling in order to make room for the expression of positive impulses, allowing for growth. When the encounter participant is rid of the dead weight of anger, remorse, inhibition, and regret he is prepared to experience hope, ambition, love, and other positive feelings that prompt maturation and new experience. The more pronounced and deep the negative expressions, once they are recognized and accepted, the more certain are the positive experiences of love, of social impulse, of self respect, and of a fundamental desire to be mature.

In encounter as in therapy, at first negative feelings emerge. Participants complain about themselves, their jobs, spouse, and friends. They pick on one another and the group and indicate their distrust and jealousy. But gradually, as the negative emotions are purged, positive feelings emerge. Of course this is not an entirely orderly process. There may well be positive feelings at the first meeting and negative ones at the nineteenth. But by and large, as negative feelings are aired and neutralized (if not entirely discarded) during the early meetings, increasingly positive ones emerge. The intensity of the feelings exposed will not (and should not) approach that of feelings exposed in psychotherapy. Encounter is a limited relationship among relatively healthy people whose purpose is not recovery from illness but self-actualization.

Reflecting

In therapy the doctor provides a climate of full acceptance and honest warmth. The patient is not judged, criticized, argued with, or challenged. Perhaps for the first time, all that he is and all he does are respected and listened to. In the same way, in encounter each person is liked and valued for himself, and he is listened to fully. In this climate of intimacy, friendship, and mutual help, genuine feelings can emerge. By attending very carefully to the words spoken and also observing tone, manner, posture, gestures, and expression, others can detect the emotion conveyed. From the total response, verbal and physical, they may deduce the feeling experienced and possibly verbalize it.

Here is an excellent example of reflection. It occurred during the fifteenth encounter session.

Sheila: I've never had any problems with sex. When I was eight I went to live with my grandfather on his farm and everything was very naturalistic. He was an old Scandinavian-type farmer and very stern but he didn't hide anything from me. I knew how the cows calved and why chickens laid eggs that were fertile. He took me for walks in the woods and showed me flowers and trees and animals and I felt very close to nature. . . . But he was very modest and would scold me, in fact punish me very badly, if I didn't sit right or wasn't modest. He was very proper and since I was the only girl in that family I was expected to be the very best of all. So I mean I accept sex; it's natural and biological and I don't put it down at all.

Mac: I get the feeling, not from what you say, but more from how you say it, that almost the opposite could be true. I may be wrong but I sense that you feel sex is somehow very improper, you know, maybe it's even all wrong. It's biological and all that but it's for animals and you feel a lot of repugnance about it. I mean how you set your face and body when you said those last few things. I mean I just had that feeling, you know.

Sheila: I don't know, Mac. (*Lengthy pause.*) I don't know. You could be right. (*Pause.*) Uh, well, let's see. Let's put it this way. I mean it's natural but that old man did manage to make me feel just living was somehow wrong. I suppose. Well you could be right. I have always recited that to myself like a prayer, I suppose, or a wish, maybe. You know. You know that sex is natural and biological but please, God, don't burden me. It's fine for others but God, I think at times I really am disgusted. Wow, I mean they really had an impact on me.

Sheila has apparently obtained a very significant insight. She had been coasting along believing her often repeated formula that she accepted sex as natural, but this was actually a defensive, emotional rationalization. Mac was able to spot her true feelings underlying her "naturalistic" description and reflect them. In this instance pointing to feeling moved Sheila forward. She was enabled to come to grips with her real sexual emotions for the first time.

Contrast that reflection with this one:

Shelly: I felt so fat being pregnant. I mean I really was so awkward. I felt off balance and my clothes wouldn't fit. And my face looked so round and swollen. I began to think maybe I should just stay home most of the time. The thing was, David did not understand at all. He was amused by it. . . . He did not seem in the slightest aware of how bad I felt or even care about it.

Tom: I think you resent David because he got you pregnant. You dislike him for it.

Shelly: Well I don't think I said that or felt that. I don't think that's true at all. I mean what I am saying is that this is a period when you are just so out of touch with your normal self, and your husband, but resentment is not how I felt. I love being pregnant and I'm looking forward to it again.

Mickey: Wow, well I've never seen you angry, Shelly, but it looks like you sure are angry at Tom.

Shelly: Well, yes. You were just so wrong [Tom], you didn't understand at all what I was saying. I'm just wondering where you're coming from.

Several differences distinguish the worthwhile and accurate reflections made by Mac (and Mickey) from the irritating comment made by Tom. Tom seems to be trying to play "psychiatrist." He listens only with the intent of commenting on another's emotional state or supposedly explaining another's action. Sooner or later he will have to come to grips with his need to play this role in encounter, for it is actually an escape for him. It is Tom's way of abstaining from participating personally, as an individual, in give-and-take intimacy with the other members.

Further, Tom's comment is "forced"—he does not actually feel the emotion that he reflected; he does not really sense that Sheila is resentful. Mac, in contrast, felt in his entire being the disgust that Sheila was conveying. The good reflection is one that a person makes honestly because his own self acts as his cue. He does not have to think long and laboriously "Now what is she feeling?" because he responds personally to the emotion being expressed.

The genuine and appropriate reflection comes from within and is partly emotional and partly intellectual. We use words to communicate the emotion we sense in the other, and those words should convey the origin of a reflection. Mac says, "I get the feeling, not from what you say, but more from how you say it . . ." and later he says, "I may be wrong but I sense. . . ." Later on Mickey says, "Well I've never seen you angry, Shelly, but it looks like you sure are angry at Tom." These statements have the quality of genuineness that Tom's comments lack. Tom is straining while Mac and Mickey are responding honestly and openly.

The first rule then for assuring that reflections are likely to be appropriate is to make certain that they genuinely communicate a person's own response. Does he really sense or feel that emotion in another? If so, then it may be useful to reflect the feeling. A second rule for reflections is to keep them scarce! By my own count, in good encounter reflections constitute about ten percent of the verbal interactions. The remaining verbal responses are agreement or restatement or (to a very, very small extent) questions and contradictions (see chapter 7). It is *not* necessary to label every emotion or reflect every nuance of feeling. Encounter is not psychotherapy and participants do not want or need to intensify an already profound experience. I often suggest that members let emotions slide by rather than reflect them. If, however, an emotional theme seems to recur and a participant has felt impelled several times to make the same reflective comment, he should.

Thus a third, informal rule for reflection is generally to avoid reflecting until the emotion has been corroborated by repetition. There is no hurry to say just the right thing at the right time. If an encounter member thinks another could benefit greatly by knowing he is angry or disgusted or jealous about something, it is usually worthwhile to wait till the feeling occurs again and then, perhaps, reflect that emotion. Similarly, participants should not feel they are in a race with one another to make just the right reflective comment. Anyone who feels he is beginning to compete with someone else to get his reflection in first should halt; he (or the other person) may be taking on the role of fraudulent group psychotherapist.

What about reflecting erroneously? A person may genuinely believe he is correct only to find the other denying the emotion.

Erna: I always thought the strongest influence on me was my mother. But maybe it was my father. I used to puzzle about my father, he used very strong discipline on me. He'd make me do what he wanted and he didn't even want to discuss it with me. Like I remember I wanted to wear penny loafers and my father made me wear saddle shoes. They were the most practical and the most obvious but I hated them. It was the same thing with the length of the dress or something, and at the time I hated it. . . . I didn't want to wear saddle shoes, everyone was wearing loafers. . . .

Laverne: Well you sound like you really resent your father.

Erna: No. I don't think so. I don't think I really feel that way. When I look back on it I didn't like it then but I think now it was really good. He made me start thinking about things like shoes and skirt lengths and wondering do you really have to do what everyone else is doing.

Mort: Yes, I think Erna is expressing a lot of good feeling towards her father, Laverne. I mean it's not immediately obvious, maybe not to you either [Erna], but I kept feeling like you really were very proud of him and had a lot of love for him.

While Erna tells Laverne that she is wrong, Erna is not angered. Laverne has made an honest and open mistake. She felt that Erna was expressing dislike of her father and she reflected this. Unlike Shelly in the previous example, in which a wrong reflection provoked anger, Erna is not distressed by the mistake because Laverne is a good encounter participant and is not trying to play the role of psychologist. She genuinely perceived this emotion and candidly pointed it out. Thus a reflection that is in error is unlikely to have any undesirable consequences if it is honest.

While a reflection may be rejected because it is wrong, it may be right and yet not be accepted. The person experiencing that feeling may not be ready to recognize it. Members may be ahead of the person, perceiving emotions he is not yet prepared to deal with. Perhaps the feeling pointed out is a threat. It may be too contrary to the person's self-image. Countless reasons may necessitate refusing a feeling when accepting it might be too painful. In the following interchange Karen is not able to agree to Wendy's reflection. To agree that she feels what Wendy describes would be too much to cope with, at this stage of her self-awareness and growth.

Karen: I never seem to be able to do anything that's right for my daughter. She's become a fanatic about horses so we were giving her lessons, but it turned out she didn't like the teacher. I mean it's the same whatever I've tried to do for her. And I don't think it's me, I have really tried, but she is exasperating.

Wendy: It looks to me, that is, whenever you talk about your daughter, Karen, I just feel all this hostility, I guess, you might call it. I mean you really seem not to like her.

Karen: Oh no, I mean I don't want to give that impression. I love my daughter. I don't dislike her at all. I mean like all children can get on your nerves sometimes. . . . A mother couldn't feel like that towards her own.

In this instance Wendy was correct. Whenever Karen complained about her daughter there was a clear undercurrent of hostility, envy, and rejection. So finally Wendy reflected the feeling. But Karen could not accept this. She was not yet prepared to deal with her hostile emotions towards her daughter. She needed to continue to live with the comforting delusion that all was completely well and that "a mother couldn't feel like that towards her own."

Another suggestion, then, for reflection is not to insist on a reflection that is rejected. First, the emotion underlined may not be correct. But more important, if the feeling pointed out is correct and is still rejected the rejection may well indicate that the person with that emotion is not yet capable of facing it. The reflected emotion that threatens and is therefore rejected must be viewed as a cue for everybody to stay away. Members should not persist. They should let the person's own positive growth forces lead him rather than attempting to manipulate and direct.

Even the reflection that is rejected because it is premature often lays a foundation or is like a seed planted for later maturation. Very frequently the feeling that is resisted is nevertheless assimilated and later comes to fruition. Andy is a good example:

You know when you said last week I was jealous, I just couldn't believe that. So I said, "Bunk." But what you said has haunted me all week and I think maybe you are right. I was just wondering about it this morning when I was talking with Lee about the car. It was like in the middle of this conversation it hit me and I said to myself, "You've just been acting jealous. That's all there is to it. You're just plain jealous." That just opened up all sorts of thoughts in me. It's a way I can explain all sorts of my feelings to myself, and really know they're true.

Group Feelings

Many of the encounter sessions, particularly the early ones, may contain a good deal of negative emotional expression. People talk about how they have been handicapped by an unhappy parental home, narrowed by life-denying moralities, disabled by the pressure of peers or authorities, and consequently grown up with all sorts of frustrations, inhibitions, and anxieties. Such past negative feelings are fairly easily accepted by the group. It is not difficult to understand or sympathize with the many ways in which someone else may have been thwarted, angered, or frightened by what others have done some time ago. But negative feelings are not all past history. As encounter progresses a good many unpleasant emotions may be found rooted in the present and particularly within the group's interaction.

When unhappy emotions include us, it may not be so easy to agree or reflect. We may even feel attacked, embarrassed, or possibly frightened. But these are emotions members must learn to accept, for inevitably encounter includes interaction that is not positive or pleasurable. Here are some examples of the ways in which a group or an individual member can become the focus of negative feelings.

Melissa: I'll be damned if I'm going to pour my heart out to a bunch of strangers who probably don't give a damn about what I'm saying. I don't think you would understand, anyway. And, anyway, I don't trust all of you. That's how I feel. I'm being honest, like it or not.

Holly: I'm sorry but I just don't like you. That's how I feel and I can't help it. You make me uneasy. You make me feel funny and I know I don't like it.

Jackie: Well I was anxious to come today, but oh no, I'm not going to be touching each other. I'm not comfortable with that, with people I don't know or may not want to know. I don't like that kind of thing and I'm not going to do it.

Richard: I think you're wrong, just plain wrong. Life is not like that and you had better learn fast. If you want to live in a dream world that's all right with me, but brother, watch out when you meet reality. I think what you people are up to is wrong and I mean wrong practically and morally. You're dead wrong and you better be prepared to take the consequences.

When members are under attack they should not be defensive, or through logic, debate, or other means attempt to point out their antagonist's error. The temptation to show that the attacker is wrong is very great, but their technique for handling negative emotion directed against them must be the same as for handling similar emotions originating in the past. They need to try sincerely to understand (agree and restate) and reflect. Negative feelings directed at them, like all other unhappy emotions, need to come to the surface and be reflected so that positive ones can grow. Here are some good reflective responses to attacks against the group or an individual. They have a genuine quality; they are not merely exercises in technique.

Sandy: I'm sorry, Jed. I feel bad that you feel so bad about me. But I am glad you said how you feel. It makes me believe you really do trust me more than you might think. It sounds like, well, you trust me enough to tell me how you feel about me, and I think that's good.

Elena: Well you're very angry at the group. You just seem madder than hell today. I wonder whether it mattered much whatever we did today, you seem so ready to be mad.

Curtis: I have had the distinct feeling this whole hour, and I have had it before, that you're really afraid of us, I feel that's what your attack is all about. You are very afraid. Well I tell you, I'll tell you honestly, that as far as I am concerned, you have absolutely nothing to fear. That's just how I feel, you're afraid and you don't have to be.

On the encouraging side it is almost certain that when negative feelings about the encounter, the participants, individuals, or the guide finally emerge, positive feelings are sure to follow. When emotional lows occur and participants become discouraged with a good deal of negative affect, they should be encouraged knowing that positive feeling is very likely to follow. Here are the words of Melissa, who only a few sessions back attacked the group.

> This is crazy but I feel so good today. I just went home last time and I said this is the most creative experience of my life. I've had this good feeling since Monday and it has not let up. I wish I could always feel like this. What I need I think is just to have you around all the time. Like Sam and what he said last time was just great. I wish he were there all the time to cheer me. I mean no one can do that but like just get into my head and see what is going on and be there and say, "You're O.K. and I think you're great." And mean it because I know he means it. It is like when Thelma said she could really love someone so much that she would want to suffer all hurt for them, forever. I think I would like Thelma to love me like that. It would be so good.

Positive Feeling

Positive feelings, like negative ones, must be reflected, in the appropriate ways. In fact some psychologists go so far as to emphasize positive emotions, rarely or never reflecting unhappy or destructive ones. The general rules for reflecting good emotions are the same as for reflecting poor ones: to make sure not to push, reflect sparingly, and reflect only when the theme has been repeated and one is personally convinced of the emotion. Here are some excellent positive reflections:

> Holly: It's just so great to be free again. At first in the two years after my husband left me I did nothing but feel sorry for myself. I was so depressed and I wouldn't even go out socially. But that was crazy. I am a big sexy girl and I love men. I'm having a ball. I'm not hung up, and I'm really beginning to enjoy life.

MaryLynn: You sound so good. You really seem to be enjoying yourself.

John: I've always wanted to build. I'm just so tired of sitting in an office all day. I just want to build a house or a barn or a chicken shed or I don't know. I don't care which. I'm just going out and do something.
Madeline: I can really feel your enthusiasm, John. You seem so happy.

A final word about positive feelings: negative ones never entirely absent themselves. Even during the last encounter meeting a few negative emotions could be expressed. Certainly there will generally be fewer and fewer as encounter progresses, but the usual encounter situation is neither long enough nor intensive enough for all negative affect to disappear. Hence in those overwhelming moments of good feeling in later encounter sessions, when all sorts of positive emotions are reflected and expressed, negative ones may reappear. We must accept good and positive emotions for themselves and recognize that though we may reduce handicapping emotions to a minimum, it is not realistic to expect ourselves or anyone else to be perfect.

Exercises

It may be worthwhile to practice reflecting. Each group participant might want to spend some time on his own, outside of the group, using reflection in situations in which he might ordinarily depend upon the give-and-take of conversation. A very amusing and rewarding series of reflections was reported by one group member. This is his description:

I was visiting my brother and I had never been there before so I wasn't familiar with his neighborhood. Anyway there was a very busy intersection with a traffic policeman and as I was coming towards him he was making these strange signals. I thought maybe he was talking to someone behind me or to the side so I just ignored him and made a left turn around him. As soon as I finished that turn, he blew his whistle, and he came running towards me, looking mad as hell and stopping all the traffic from all directions.

So I pulled over and he stuck his head in the window and he said something like "What the hell do you think you're doing. You're looking right at me, and you seen me signal. What are you up to, Mister?" Well I decided to reflect. "I'm sorry, officer, I can understand that you must be very angry at me." He said, "You're damned right. Didn't you see that sign, I pointed right at it, for you." So I said again, "It must be very frustrating to have so many people like me not seeing obvious traffic signs."

Meanwhile he had his ticket book out and was beginning to fill in the date but he stopped after my second reflection and looked at me. I think he said then, "I can't believe you didn't see that no left turn sign and my direction both." I just reflected, "You're doubtful that I missed both those obvious signs." So he said something to the effect that he was doubtful and then he went on that I seemed a reasonable person and not someone trying to get away with something. I reflected some more and before you know it we were talking about how I was just a visitor here and how I had to be more careful and he let me off without a ticket.

There is absolutely no guarantee that reflection is the way to avoid traffic tickets. But new insight into the way in which people get along results when we attempt reflection in situations in which we might normally converse or argue. Here are some circumstances in which it might be appropriate to attempt reflection:

1. discussion with a child
2. learning about someone's ethnic biases
3. dispute about political issues
4. buying an appliance, automobile or other large item
5. getting to know someone new at a party

On rare occasions, when an encounter group seems puzzled or confused about identifying emotions, the group might try a joint literary exercise. Passages are read from a novel or transcripts are read from other encounters; participants write down and later discuss jointly the emotions conveyed. There will not always be total agreement, but this is a good way for all participants to heighten their sensitivity to their own and others' feelings.

Chapter 7

Questions, Contradictions, and Anger

Every honest conversation, even when mutual understanding and rapport are maximal, contains an occasional question. What's more, no matter how genuinely we may feel with another, there are times when we cannot avoid contradicting what he is saying or experiencing. In the same way, during encounter there will be periods when a question has to be asked and perhaps a disagreement voiced. In my experience, in a good group interaction, in which members feel close and are productive, questions and contradictions are very infrequent. My own informal count suggests that the great majority of encounter responses are agreement or restatement. A small proportion of comments are reflection (chapter 6) or feedback (chapter 9) or their equivalent. The least frequent comments, perhaps about five percent, are outright interrogations or contradictions. Group members or guides need not actually tally their comments, of course. Further, in any one session there may be considerable deviation from these figures. But these numerical approximations should help participants sense if they are questioning too much, restating too little, or otherwise differing markedly from other growth encounter groups.

In certain instances questions are appropriate and valuable. During the fourth meeting of a group that seemed headed in the right direction, a participant said:

> Maybe this is too early to say this but I get the impression that just a few of us are carrying the ball. Like Darlene and Yolanda have said a lot about themselves and like a lot of others haven't said anything, hardly. . . . I was just wondering, or maybe it makes me feel uneasy, why some of us, like Shirley and Keith, haven't said much at all. I'd like to ask, maybe, uh, why are you so quiet? Are you holding back?

The question *Why*, when some participants are willing to risk revealing themselves, do others hold back? is often a good one. This is the kind of challenge frequently required in early encounter sessions to help prod those that are reluctant or reserved to come forth and disclose something of themselves. It would be unfair, possibly even unethical, to permit a few encounter members to sit passively, learning about the lives of others without themselves making any commitment. The question Why are you not participating? focuses directly on this very meaningful group concern.

When someone is asked about his lack of participation it is often the only additional impetus needed to help him get started. Such a gentle question, coming at the right time, may make the difference. Granted, sometimes an inquiry about non-involvement leads to a decision to quit the group. This too is a valuable function of a proper question. Often people start with a group but have serious doubts that they are ready for such an experience. Persons like this tend to sit back, withholding themselves, while they try to resolve their ambivalence. A valid inquiry at the crucial moment helps them decide whether to go ahead and jump in or get off the diving board. It is entirely legitimate (and frequently commendable) for a beginning participant to decide that the encounter experience is not what he needs or wants and leave the group. In fact, dur-

ing the early sessions, particularly, members should be continuously encouraged to think over whether they should remain, withdraw, or consider some alternative to encounter to
enhance their lives.

A second instance in which questions may be very worthwhile is when there is no other way in which members can
deepen their understanding of one another. Perhaps they have
restated what has been said and sought insight by reflection,
but they still do not understand. Then a question may certainly be in order.

Glenn: It is like I was saying before, I do not like to be dominated. I do not care who it is. Like it could be my little
daughter and she'll say play with me, or my wife, she says
she wants me to do this or that. . . . We were at this party
and she said let's dance. And I said no, man, I have to feel
in the mood. . . . I am not going to dance unless I feel like
it. . . . And then Janis is telling me that I come on strong,
but I am just telling her that I am going to do this my own
way.
Stuart: Glenn, are you saying that you feel we, here, push you
around?
Glenn: Well if you want a point-blank answer then I will say,
Yeah, I do feel you are. . . . I am not saying you are trying
to push me around, but you all have an idea of what you
want me to do and I may not want to do it. . . .
Edna: I understand Glenn, he feels a sort of group consensus
on what is expected. . . .
Glenn: Right. . . .
Edna: But it would really help me if you told what you felt
we were doing. Could you sort of just let your feelings out,
I mean how am I or Stu or somebody else coming on that
you feel dominated?
Glenn: Right, okay. Now I'll tell you what I mean. . . .

In this instance several questions, motivated by members'
desire to comprehend Glenn more fully, encourage Glenn to

there may be considerable deviation from these figures. But these numerical approximations should help participants sense clarify his situation for himself. The questions based on one participant's lack of understanding often simultaneously help another move ahead in his own feelings and thoughts.

All the occasions and motives that warrant a question cannot be detailed. In nearly every encounter session a few situations almost demand at least some degree of questioning comment. One other good reason to question is that a question can be a way of "floating an idea." Occasionally members may have an insight, about themselves or about another, or may have some suggestion for the group, but they are not certain. They want to examine the notion—perhaps it is right, wrong, or partially correct in some way. A good way to do this is to state the hunch tentatively. Here are several such interrogative statements:

I've heard Frances say that before and I always wonder whether it is actually jealousy and not just her achievement needs, like she says, that makes her do it. I wonder if maybe anyone has the same feeling? I could be wrong.

I was tossing around yesterday if we should spend more time talking about our relationships with the opposite sex. I think we talked a lot about what we want to do but we forgot how much of our lives we are doing things together with our partner, whether we are married or just living together or whatever. I was thinking whether we should spend a few sessions just concentrating on how we are working things out with our wives, or husbands, friends or whatever. . . . I'm not sure we ought to do this, but I was thinking I should raise this to see how the rest of you feel. Do you think it makes any sense, or what?

Have you ever thought that we should all live together? I'm serious. I keep getting the idea that this shouldn't end. I know it is not the usual ending, and maybe it never happens at all. But maybe we should really talk about it. Should we all live together?

Contradicting

Even when questions are good, fully appropriate and necessary, in total they still occupy a relatively small area of all
verbal exchange. Even less frequent are contradictions. On
rare occasions it may be to the point to disagree or otherwise
highlight an inconsistency in another's narration. The rules
for good contradiction are very similar to those for valid
questioning. A statement of disagreement may be helpful when
it *acts as a beneficial stimulant, deepens understanding,* or
otherwise *moves individuals or the group forward.* An additional rule, which should be apparent from the previous examples, is that questions and contradictions should never
emerge from hostile motives. When members are angered by
another's comments or story, an interrogation or disagreement
is rarely if ever appropriate. Instead of attacking, it is usually
best to state frankly that what another has said has caused
some uneasiness, anxiety, or other unpleasant emotion. This
permits all concerned to examine the feelings revealed without feeling attacked, being defensive, or otherwise trying to
justify their positions.

Jenny: The more you talked, Paul, the more it disturbed me.
I didn't want to interrupt you but I kept feeling like I should
almost shout, "Why, why are you saying that about your
mother? How do you know that's what went on with your
father?" I recognize your feelings really touched a raw
nerve in me. I got very upset. But I don't really know myself why I respond that way. . . . I still feel a little upset but
I feel better telling you how you made me feel. . . .
Sal: You do seem to be a lot better. You looked very angry,
like you were holding it all in, now you look better.
Jenny: I felt like attacking Paul but as I held back I started
to understand why I overreact like that whenever the subject of parents comes up. I still don't think I agree with
Paul's feelings but I am beginning to understand myself. I
keep putting myself in their place. . . .

Questions and contradictions that do not emerge from negative drives but reflect attempts at encouragement, clarification, and progress are almost always phrased in a somewhat hesitant, tentative, and non-demanding manner. These questions and contradictions are nearly as much an examination of the questioner as they are of another. He is not trying to put another member on the spot but is offering assistance that is gentle and caring.

Dot: It's very easy to get angry and just scream at people and don't give a damn what they think when you scream at them. But when I moved in with Billy, living in a different type of situation, with someone that you really live close with and things come up where you did feel kind of annoyed, I tried to control myself because you just can't have fights with people. Sometimes you just have to make the living conditions more comfortable. . . . I sort of, after three years, I've sort of controlled it to a certain degree. So when I go home now I don't get into fights with my family very much. You know I don't get angry now at all. Only when they really do something really stupid. . . .

Lee: You only get angry when they do something really dumb. I used to get angry at little situations like I'd be drying my blouse in the shower and it'd be hanging there and someone would take a shower and close the curtain and crush my blouse up. And when they finished and pulled the curtain back they wouldn't fix my blouse. I'd get angry at things like that. But now instead of getting angry I just fix my blouse and say, "Hey stupid, cut it out, you should fix it after you're finished taking a shower." So like I do things like that all the time, now. When I get annoyed I say something to the other person instead of just getting angry. . . .

Dot: Uh huh. . . . Those are the kind of things I've learned to control, little things that come up in the course of contact. You know bigger things it takes longer. . . . It takes longer to get angry and it takes longer to get out from the anger. I used to get into angry things like where I wouldn't talk to somebody, like my father I wouldn't talk to him for months, and we lived in the same house. . . . Can you imagine? . . . When I get angry I get very cold, and I don't think I am a very cold person. But I don't have those problems now. I don't get angry anymore.

Dan: You know [Lee], I'm sitting here and I listen to you but I'm not sure I get the feeling your words are saying. I mean your words and your actions, maybe, might be quite different. It just hit me when you said about your blouse you don't get angry, you just say something like "Hey stupid, cut it out, fix it before you leave the shower," or something. You were saying that's how you don't get angry but you said that so loud and strong that . . . that is what I could, possibly, call an angry response. . . . You know what I mean? I'm not really sure of my own feeling here, but I sort of sense you might not actually be aware of how angry you still are. You may think that you don't have problems with being really mad anymore but from the way you've described things I don't know whether that's the entire picture. : . . Well that's how it struck me . . . sort of my gut feeling to your emotions more than your words. I don't know if I'm on the right track at all. . . .

Lee: No, I can see that. I don't know. . . . I'm not saying I don't have any of that kind of feeling anymore. . . . I thought I was over more of it than it showed, I guess.

Most contradictive comments, like Dan's, point to inconsistencies, rationalizations, or conflicts in another's self-description or narrative. They contrast what the speaker is supposedly revealing or experiencing with what he actually reveals about himself now or in other sessions. When such self-contradictions are pointed out reasonably, they help the individual obtain new understanding and otherwise integrate his feelings.

Sometimes contradictions can be simple, outright disagreements. One group member may feel quite differently about an interpretation, experience, belief, or value. Members may disagree about a number of topics and it may be worthwhile to air such opposing views.

I can't entirely agree with you, Beth. You keep saying how you can't have sex with someone you don't know. How you're supposed to have a relationship first, and how you're supposed to feel something for that person. Like otherwise it's supposed to be just an animal thing, and you seem to assume we more or less all agree with you. But I don't quite agree. Sex is good and it can be good in different ways. . . . Sometimes you want to get to know someone first. Like you say, and I agree, you want their personality or their feelings for you to turn you on. But I think that's not all there is. Like sometimes you just meet someone and say, "Wow, I'd love to get them in bed," and you don't know them very much or feel very deeply at all. And that kind of one-night stand can be very good for both of you. . . . I believe it's just putting down sex saying you must, it's required you know somebody and like somebody and all that. I mean if you say that's the only way then it's just bull, because sex is good without that too. Anyone that's open to sex knows that; they've found it out. It can be just a lovely act of casual friendship the way you might really enjoy talking to someone next to you for several hours on a plane trip and never see them again.

I personally don't like the way you always seem to put down America. I understand how you feel about it and I could see how you came to be like that. But when you often seem to slip in some derogatory comment about our system, a lot of the time I think you're wrong. . . . You haven't been outside the U.S.A. otherwise you'd know the difference. We have all sorts of things wrong here I grant you, but compared to anywhere else this is still a pretty remarkable country.

I am sorry to disagree with Howard and Jan but honestly they're both wrong. I am not trying to act superior to women. I have worked my relationship through my own mind, very, very often and I honestly believe I have no need to be dominating. I will agree I get anxious, or even plain scared, or I act childish, but I don't feel anywhere in my bones any desire to manipulate. I just don't think, honestly, you are interpreting me correctly.

Needless to say, questions and contradictions are not always as scarce as they ought to be, nor as constructively motivated. A good encounter interaction can withstand some friction and even occasional negative contributions. But a growth group should not and cannot persist in the face of vituperation, cross-examination, inquisition, and manipulation. The more members argue and attack the more likely the group will be damaged and eventually even dissolve in acrimony. Here is a segment of a dispute which recurred so frequently that the group dissolved with considerable bitterness.

Art: I agree, most men do cheat on their wives. It's sort of natural you might almost say.

Ron: What do you mean most? Do you have any figures on that?

Art: Well I don't know, it's what you read in the papers and magazines.

Nina: I think that what Art is saying is that it is his experience that makes him believe most men cheat.

Art: Yes, hm mm.

Ron: When you say "most" you are making a statistical statement and you have to back it up. How do you know, Nina, that it is his experience he is talking about? What kind of evidence do you have?

Sandy: What're you so up-tight about? I think most men cheat too.

Ron: You're wrong! That's all. Most men don't cheat unless you have facts to prove otherwise.

Art: I read that 60% of all married men cheat at least once.

Ron: Where did you read that?

Art: In the *News*.

Ron: When, what edition?

Art: Last Sunday, I think.

Ron: Who reported the figures? Who collected them? How

did they find out?

Art: I don't remember all that. I think it was some psychiatrist writing.

Ron: Who was he? Do you trust the *News*? Is that a reliable paper?

Art: I don't remember every name, and it's a paper like any other.

Ron: Now you don't remember any names, nor who was surveyed, nor how the survey was done, nor what they asked and you expect us to believe you. I am asking you, all of you, do we believe this, on this basis?

Nina: Who do you think you are, Perry Mason? It's what he believes, he feels it. . . .

Sandy: Stop all this bull! Why [Ron] do you care about the numbers? What business is it of yours?

Pete: If this is the kind of bull that's going to go on here I might as well go down to the corner bar. They may argue like this but at least you get a drink with it.

In summary, the guidelines for keeping questions and contradictions constructive center about motivation. Cross-examination, rebuttal, and verbal contests are not likely to result if inquiries or disagreements are positively motivated. My personal rule, when I feel inclined to probe or dispute, is to ask myself if I am convinced my verbal intrusion will really be helpful. As a consequence I make far fewer comments than I feel tempted to make. By exercising restraint and keeping in mind the necessity for helping others grow, members can ensure that whatever questions and contradictions do emerge are likely to be worthwhile.

Handling Anger

The nature of the verbal processes I suggest and those I restrict may have given the reader the impression that what takes place in growth encounter is a goody-goody, otherworldly sort of mutual admiration. There is a kernel of truth in this impression, for one of the purposes of encounter is to demonstrate how well people can function in a warm and help-ful atmosphere. Personal growth and continued maturation do not require fearful stress or shattering conflict but are encour-aged most in a beneficent milieu.

But is it not being dishonest to suppress a question or con-tradiction? Is it not a lack of genuineness and spontaneity to divert the urge to inquire and argue? "I won't feel right re-straining myself." "It isn't sincere for me not to contradict." "Aren't we supposed to let it all hang out?" The answer to these questions is that members do not let "hang out" that which is really an assault upon another. Yes, they frankly re-veal their frustrations, helplessness, and other unhappy emo-tions, but this openness is not a license to strike out at others. They are not being dishonest when they suppress their aggres-sion, violence, and misanthropy, for an ancillary purpose of encounter is to teach them to overcome anger.

To grow as humane beings we need to become alert to how often our negative and hostile feelings subvert our potential and stifle our development. People meet in encounter not to replay and repeat all the aggressive and hate-filled behaviors they have been taught all their lives but to learn new ways of relating to one another. In encounter they are presented the opportunity to unlearn envy, negativism, and pugnacity and replace them with concern and acceptance. When Ron cross-examined Art about his statement that most husbands are unfaithful to their wives, Art's description apparently made Ron very uncomfortable. But instead of addressing his own discomfort he attacked Art. Contrast Ron's hostile reaction with the response in this exchange:

Peg: My husband has had affairs, if you want to call it that. But I'm not upset like you are supposed to be. I know it doesn't mean anything's wrong between us. Lots of hus-bands, and wives too, most of them do something extra-curricular now and then.

Penny: I know, you've said that before, Peg. And I'm not sure I could take it like you do. And I'm not sure you're right that most husbands and wives actually do that. It makes me very uneasy to think about that whole area. And I don't think it's just jealousy. Maybe it's my old puritanism rearing its head. . . . I believe, I like to believe, that most couples are very faithful. . . . We are, I know it. . . . But . . . I suppose I wish I could feel more open to it, like you do. Instead, I guess, to tell the truth, I feel very sad, sometimes I feel pretty mad even, when you talk like that. I think it is kind of a challenge to me directly. . . . I know you are not saying this to me directly, and you are not saying these things to make me uncomfortable but it happens anyway. . . . I think what I'm saying is . . . that is a topic where I'm scared. I think I'd like to be able to try it but I'm very frightened. I think that's one of my feelings, just fright. Does that make any sense?

What a world of difference between Penny's response and that of Ron. Penny felt anger too, but instead of lashing out and vigorously cross-examining Peg, trying to make her squirm, she has analyzed the sources of her emotion. She has curbed her acrimony and tried to dig behind her initial response of discomfort and annoyance.

Learning positive responses and being helpful is not easy. We have been taught enmity, thrusting and destroying. When we are uncomfortable, frustrated, or confused we react offensively with opposition and malice. From infancy on, our most negative tendencies are encouraged. Parents, authorities, the so-called entertainment media, our entire social structure continuously provide example after example and even hearty commendation for every malevolent and destructive tendency. I do not believe, however, that man is predestined to be endlessly combative or that we cannot consciously alter some of our behavior. If aggressive tendencies are indeed innate to a degree, it is equally likely that altruistic potential is also inborn. The important question, therefore, is not what we are born with but which traits are cultivated and which are discouraged. In much of our lives animosity is rewarded, but in growth encounter affection, good will, and regard should be reinforced. This attitude was summarized very well by one successful encounter participant, who put it this way:

> I think one of the most valuable things I have learned is that anger is never a worthwhile alternative. What I mean by that is that when something happens to you and you get angry that anger is the least likely, of all the possible responses, to get you what you wanted in the first place. Say like you hear something in the group, and you're upset. . . . Should you let them have it, really hit back or storm out in anger, or talk over why you feel this way . . . why did this happen to me. . . . Or something else like the plumber doesn't show up. Should you yell at him, or try to understand his problems and work together for a new time. Or your wife forgets to type an important letter for you, should you be angry with her or find out what happened . . . what could have caused it. . . . Of all the things you can do when something happens that makes you angry the least likely reaction to solve anything, to get you what you want in the first place, is anger.

That statement was worth repeating, for it is an important lesson to be learned from encounter. Anger-motivated questions, comments, and behavior are more than likely to lead any relationship to a dead end. In contrast actions and responses that are open, sympathetic, and understanding often overcome frustration and anxiety, mobilize creativity, and lead to constructive growth.

Exercises

Some groups may need to practice questioning and contradicting at various stages of encounter. In early stages some people may be so reluctant to risk upsetting others that they never query or oppose statements. Later in encounter, and at the opposite extreme, those accustomed to do almost nothing but question and oppose tend to surface. They are so used to resisting in a habitually negative manner that they are no longer comfortable with ordinary agreeable conversation.

Questioning exercises obviously help the former group learn to overcome their timidity. How does the latter group benefit? Those who are negativistically inclined are used to disputing in an almost reflexive manner. But in these exercises they will have to give considerable thought to choosing every question and measuring the appropriate timing for every contradiction. Further, they will be made aware of their need to interject. Ultimately, with the help of other participants, they will be able to see the difference between negativistic opposition and queries based on a sincere need to know or clarify a situation.

The Source of Authority

All of us have beliefs, values, justifications, and opinions about a huge variety of issues and conduct. In this exercise encounter members are asked to state a disapproving judgment and make explicit their source of authority for that view. Other members then ask questions in order to deepen their own understanding and to make as clear as possible the basis for that view. Here is an example:

Hal: I believe that homosexuality is wrong and sick and I base my view on the Bible.

Rita: What is there in the Bible that makes you say that, Hal?

Hal: I can't quote you chapter and verse but it says in many places something like if a man be with a man it is an abomination . . . they are stoned or cast out. . . .

Oscar: Do you believe everything in the Bible? Do you believe Adam and Eve, for example, or the story about Jonah and the whale? . . .

Hal: Well . . . well of course not . . . but the Bible contains much truth. . . . It is the distillation of the wisdom of ages . . . and homosexuality is obviously wrong . . . men and women were made for each other. . . .

Rita: Then to be really honest, Hal, you don't base you belief about homosexuality being wrong on the Bible entirely; you think—you just feel that it is wrong. Your own feeling here is the source of authority. . . .

Tanna: Be honest, Hal, it is your own feeling here, or you
could even say your own bias, isn't it?

Hal: Well maybe it could be, but I do believe in God and I
think He does not approve of homosexuality.

Dan: Wow, that's quite a statement. How do you know He
does not approve? What is your source for saying that?

Exercises in learning to question also provide an opportunity for the persons being questioned to handle themselves
in such situations. The preceding dialog makes it apparent
that defending one's beliefs can be a trying experience. But it
is far less stressful as an exercise than when one member is the
subject of another's malevolent cross-examination, as in the
case of Ron vs. Art. The following exchange is another example of an exercise in perceptive questioning. It also illustrates that while the questioners must espouse *positive* motives,
the person being examined must be totally *honest*.

Marcy: I firmly believe dope addicts should be severely punished, put in jail for life, maybe. This nation has the right
to defend itself. The law is my authority.

Frank: Why? Couldn't what you call the law sometimes be
wrong?

Marcy: No, the law is right. The dope pushers are wrong because they ruin their lives and they ruin other people's lives;
they steal and they mug people.

David: What kind of dope are you talking about?

Marcy: All kinds of dope.

David: Well marijuana is not the same as heroin, is it?

Marcy: Well it may not be at the beginning but they go on and
on and before you know it they are dope addicts and steal-
ing and murdering. . . .

Pat: This is not getting us anywhere. I would like to know
why you [Marcy] feel so strongly about this when you seem
to know so little. . . .

Marcy: It is true that I don't know much about it but the whole
idea disgusts me. . . . And young people today have such

disgusting habits about them ... they're not clean ... and that's part of my whole feeling.

Allison: So you might say that you reject these people and their habits because you don't like them? It's not the law, it's more that you don't like them.

Marcy: Well you could say it that way ... to be very honest with myself.

Allison: Have you ever thought why you don't like them, what is there really deep down in yourself that makes you feel disgusted?

Marcy: I don't know, to tell the truth, it's the way I grew up probably, my parents, I suppose, but I don't know yet where those kinds of feelings come from. They're very strong, I know that, but I'll have to be in this group a lot longer before I figure out why I have such very strong feelings of dislike for different things. I do want to be a more tolerant person.

In addition to its usefulness in the area of questioning, the Source of Authority exercise may occasionally be used to initiate encounter sessions. The new members, together for the first time, are instructed to examine the question of authority. Who decides what is right and what is proper? On what basis shall we judge whether a behavior is good or bad, sick or healthy? What are our goals and who is to decide whether we have met them or not? Such questions, and all that flows from them, can be an excellent way of getting individuals to start thinking about their own beliefs and bringing them together to function as a group.

Impact

A second exercise that may be useful, particularly during the early stages of encounter, teaches individuals and the group the potency of words. It may be well to couple the authority questions and impact exercises; the Source of Authority exercise makes plain how much discomfort questions and contradictions may cause. The impact exercise is designed to demonstrate the varying effects of assertive statements. Each member is asked to say something that will have a measurable impact on others: to please, or shock, or make them envious or proud of us. The statement must be true but may be exaggerated to maximize its potency. After each statement the members tell how the statement affected them, and the one who made the statement reveals what he hoped its impact would be. A discussion may then follow as to why some members reacted with envy, say, while others were shocked, and as to the original intentions of the member who made the statement. Here are some statements made by encounter members, with their impact given in parentheses:

I have known you all for two weeks, and you see me as a nice twenty-eight-year-old mother, pretty conventional, but I want you all to know that I am a nudist. I have been going to nudist camps and parks since I was nineteen. (*Intended effect was shock; but several members reacted with pleasure, one person with pride, another with surprise, and another was envious.*)

I want you all to know that I really love you all, every one of you. I really have gotten to love you. (*Intended effect was pleasure; but a few members reacted with hostility and similar feelings.*)

Whenever I come here I get turned on. I'd like to make it with Celia, Debbie, and Nicky. I'd like to right here. Why not? I think we should have an orgy. (*Intended effect was shock; but there was also pleasure, hostility, disgust, and sexual excitement.*)

I mean what I am going to say. So watch out! I think you're all a bunch of phonies. Pseudo-intellectual creeps that should be working harder to make a decent living, instead of sitting around here and running off at the mouth. (*Intended effect was hostility; but there was also anxiety, disappointment, surprise, and confusion.*)

Homework

Some encounter participants like to try exercises outside

the group occasionally. As already mentioned, in some circumstances reflecting and restating can facilitate ordinary conversation. In a more limited way, questioning and contradicting in order to get at and evaluate the source of authority may occasionally be worthwhile. It may both sharpen the encounter members' perceptiveness and add to the understanding of the non-encounter participant being examined. Carefully done, such questioning may help spread more enlightened and tolerant attitudes. Of course, since this "exercise" is being conducted outside the group, relatively experienced encounter members are required. They must be extraordinarily careful and sympathetic, to minimize any anxiety they may arouse in the other. Impact statements do not transfer well. Sometimes the understanding members get of the potency of words may make them more effective speakers or conversationalists; but impact, like other exercises, should essentially be confined to encounter groups.

Chapter 8

Involving the Body

Encounter has traditionally included body activities. Consequently most encounter members expect to spend some time touching, being lifted, and otherwise involving themselves physically. But touch, sensory, and other body exercises are not indispensable to growth groups. When an interaction is going very well, with participants feeling increasingly warm and understanding, contact activity may not be needed. In fact, introducing touch tasks might even be an unproductive intrusion on the atmosphere of an ongoing group. Body involvement is not an automatic accompaniment of encounter simply because people erroneously expect all groups to do something physical.

In addition to contact tasks' being used because of false expectations or for their superficial entertainment value, body activities may also be used because they supposedly condense the dynamics of encounter. "Trust" walks, in which members lead each other around blindfolded, are said to be a shortcut in developing person-to-person honesty and dependence.

Wrestling may be staged, allegedly to provide insight and acceptance of violent feelings. Thoroughgoing man-woman body touch explorations are reputed to smash inhibitory barriers and liberate the libido. To some extent all such activities may help, but they should not be thought of as either guaranteed aids or shortcuts. There is no way of "instantizing" the encounter process. The work of encounter is primarily verbal, and no substitute is available. Further, physical activities should be only a small part of encounter, lest all that members eventually recall from their sessions are a number of amusing touch situations that had little longterm benefit.

Some types of body involvement may be useful in growth groups during early sessions. In the beginning stages of encounter some elementary touch activities can act as icebreakers, enabling members to speak familiarly and openly. Having touched one another, they feel closer and a little more confidently at ease. During later encounter sessions, perhaps around the middle of the series of meetings, body contact may also be worthwhile to bring relief from too much talk, too much intellectualizing and theorizing. As one participant put it, "There's been so much head activity here I feel as if the rest of me doesn't exist anymore." At this level, too, touch can facilitate the group's growing relationship. Besides bringing verbally overtired participants back to earth, body involvement can help them tune in a little better to themselves and others and can round out the interaction.

Other occasions when touch may be useful arise when group or environmental conditions seem to demand it. Group conditions may include, for example, a gathering of adolescents. They may be bursting with energy and need some activity to relieve the monotony of sitting and talking hour after hour. Older people too many need periods to stretch, perhaps to massage and otherwise relieve their stiffness. Or perhaps group members may express directly their desire to experience one another physically, to complement their emotional and intellectual rapport. They want to hug one another or otherwise manifest their growing feeling of closeness. They want and need some body experience to actualize new levels in their relationship.

Some environmental conditions seem naturally and obviously to call for contact exercises. A group meeting in the summer should not feel continuously frustrated by being shut indoors but might be encouraged to have a few sessions, with some physical involvement, outdoors. A group meeting at the "Y" or similar facility might make use of the gym, if members seem to express such needs. In summary, the activities encouraged should grow out of the needs of the group and their situation. They should not be intrusive or diversionary but should contribute to the purpose of the encounter.

Touch, Sex, and Fear

Obvious sexual connotations adhere to embracing, body manipulation, and other contacts that can occur during encounter physical activities. Since society generally views sexual expression negatively, many participants may be very frightened of making physical contact with a member of the opposite sex: it suggests all sorts of impropriety or precipitates feelings of personal inadequacy. While all members may be fearful, married persons in particular may become so conflict-filled that they suffer considerable distress. They very much want to show their tender feelings towards others and be touched or held, yet the rigidity of their background or views makes them feel immensely guilty. While not all participants have serious touch-anxiety, all members are likely to feel some unease; body activities should be started very slowly, gradually, and carefully.

In a group that was beginning body involvement with hugging, one member, Gil, seemed uneasy. He sat quietly and distantly for a while and then began to object to the exercise. He stated that he thought hugging was forced, artificial, and even downright childish or silly. While these arguments might have made some sense quite early in the encounter, when hugging might have been out of place, the entire group now seemed ready to get closer and express themselves physically. But Gil continued to object until one member apparently accurately caught the anxiety underlying Gil's reservations:

Sara: Gil, I get the feeling you would be personally uncomfortable embracing . . . you don't seem to think it is proper or something.

Gil: It's not proper . . . proper is not the word . . . I don't think. . . . What it is, is that it is not part of the commitment I made. I'll put it this way . . . I agreed with my wife before I ever came here that this would not be one of those groups you read about that ends up with all this hanky-panky. I feel I would be violating my wife's trust if I started fooling around by embracing everybody.

Jed: But this is confidential, Gil, nobody will know and besides it's not sex to give somebody a bear hug.

Gil: It is sex, and I would know, and my wife does know that Becky is part of this group and Becky is very young and is very attractive. . . .

Sara: So you feel that you would feel guilty especially because your wife knows about Becky who is very attractive.

Gil: It's not that I don't want to. . . . I want to get closer to all of you . . . you mean a lot to me and I'm trying . . . but I have to fight how I feel inside.

As the discussion grew and other members indicated their understanding Gil increasingly revealed how very frustrated he felt. His relationship with his wife was apparently highly confining both sexually and emotionally. He felt nearly as guilty liking or being liked by the others as he did touching them. The suggestion to embrace had simply served to focus all sorts of affectional as well as sexual conflicts and frustrations.

As Gil probed deeper within himself he became more and more emotional, revealing the depths of his misery, and finally began to cry. With his tears Gil's voice dropped to a whisper, and when he was barely audible he seemed to be mumbling his need for love. At this point one of the older women in the group went over to him and cradled his head in her arms as she gently rocked back and forth. Soon a few other members joined in and held Gil's hands or arms, demonstrating their concern and warmth. The wordless physical contact continued for some time until Gil looked up, repeated "Thank you" again and again, and went to each participant in turn, hugging each tenderly and generously.

One does not relieve fear about touch by falsely asserting that physical contact is not sexual. Of course there is sensual pleasure in tenderly touching another and being touched in return. The difference, however, between touch in a valid encounter situation and touch which has direct sexual meaning is one of purpose. Outside a growth group touch may be used to begin sexual intimacy between partners, or it may be part of the ritualistic, dead-end flirtation that is so common at parties and social gatherings. During encounter touch is not used to deliberately excite, manipulate, or pursue any of the chase-and-tease sexual games that are such an unfortunate part of our everyday lives. Growth participants engage their physical beings to learn about each other and themselves. Their contact is mutually enjoyable, but it is also a step forward in the group relationship. In the words of one member, "Touch is a way of talking that goes beyond words."

A common false perception about encounter is that there is nudity, with or without body contact. Newspaper and magazine reports picture groups standing naked in a pool or running unclothed along a beach. Whatever the value of nudity (and there may be considerable value) in our erotically repressive society, most members are not likely to be comfortable unclothed. Thus, while some so-called nude encounters could be worthwhile under excellent professional circumstances, nudity is generally a distraction in growth groups. For body activities, as for the entire encounter itself (see chapter 2, "Participants and Setting"), members should wear clothing of the type used for relaxation or lounging. However, at home with a spouse, or some other partner not from the group, members could try some body activities unclothed. This is frequently a pleasant and informative adjunct to the encounter experience.

A final warning about body exercises is that they must not become so routine that spontaneity is erased. Activities should usually be introduced in a tentative, loosely structured manner, letting the current needs of the growth group give them their final shape. In fact, in many good groups members do not wait for the formal introduction of contact activities. They will already have held hands or hugged one another with genuine feelings of closeness. Such groups may even invent their own activities and avoid formal body exercises. Groups should not feel obligated to engage in any contact events at all; they should also feel free to pick, choose, and modify any and all of the techniques discussed in the following pages.

Holding Hands, Hugging

We have learned to express our affection by embracing others. When positive feelings between members in the growth group have become evident, it may be worthwhile to try this simplest of all touch exercises. Encounter members might begin with meaningful handholding and handshaking. Members are encouraged to take each other's hand, hold it, squeeze it, and shake it to indicate as much warmth and feeling as they possibly can. When hands touch, communicating mutual interest and depth, the urge to take hold of the other person's arm and to give an amicable hug soon follows. All encounter members might be encouraged to try this sequence with everyone else in the group, men and women. Incidentally, hugging may become so common that participants frequently embrace one another at the beginning and end of sessions. Sometimes members may also want to hold hands, particularly during trying times, to indicate their encouragement and concern or express their need and trust of one another.

Music and Dance

Musical activities and dancing are excellent ways of loosening a group. There may be occasions when members want very much to start some sort of contact but still feel too many inhibitory barriers to attempt something as direct as hugging.

Dance and music may be very useful in such situations but need not be limited to them. Both dance and music may be used in countless variations. Here are some activities I have found useful:

1. Gentle rhythmic music is played (for instance a waltz or ballad) and members are asked to keep time to the music individually by swaying, moving their arms or feet, or moving their whole bodies. After a while they are encouraged to walk about and loosen up in time with the music. ("Go with the music. . . . Keep time with your head and shoulders. . . . Now let your arms join in. . . . Move your fingers.")

2. More vigorous rock-type music may be played to encourage participants to move with greater feeling. Spontaneity and improvisation are encouraged, and members make up their own steps and activities.

3. Groupings and partnerships are suggested. Members look around and try to coordinate some of their movements, improvised or otherwise, with one or more other encounter participants. When this is well done, several groups of two and three or four synchronize their actions with each other.

4. After rest periods and breaks, which should be scattered throughout music and dance activities, close groupings may be tried. Members form a circle and place their arms around each other's waists. Soft music is played and the group sways and hums along. Each is then asked to form a partnership with the person next to him and dance with that person in the old contact style. This activity should be continued for half an hour to an hour with frequent changing of partners in some arbitrary manner (for instance, changing to the person nearest when the music stops) so that nearly every participant will have danced with every other participant. (One participant commented, "I never thought old-fashioned dancing could be a growth experience.")

5. On rare occasions some musical games may be appropriate. Members may be asked to imitate the walk and bearing of some animal in time with the music. Another activity requires participants to imagine they are struggling their way into some massive "glob," also in time with music. In another game members are asked to mirror and/ or imitate each other's movements, including facial expressions, in musical rhythm. These and similar activities have some pure enjoyment value, but their primary purpose is to bring participants closer and help stimulate freer interactions.

Body Sounds

There are many different ways in which we can, by ourselves or with the help of another, become more directly conscious of our own and others' bodies. One common technique is for members to listen to each other's body noises. One member lies face upward while the other sits bent at his side, with his ear against the other's stomach. The stomach noises are listened to and reported. Members then change places. Breathing, heart sounds, and other body noises can also be listened to. In another activity participants take each other's pulse at the wrist, forehead, and neck, and explore to discover where else a pulse sound can be detected. This is followed by attempts to speed up or slow down the pulse. One member imagines a very peaceful or exciting scene and the partner reports whether the pulsebeat has been successfully decreased or increased. Partners tell each other their feelings about becoming aware of their own and the other's body.

Touching, Stretching, Massaging

Touch exercises can help heighten awareness, harmonize physical and emotional needs, and bring encounter participants closer. One participant may touch another while the latter has his eyes closed. The one touching may begin by gently feeling the other's head. For example, fingers are run lightly and slowly through the hair to feel its thickness and origin, the ears are carefully felt, and the nose and eyes subtly probed. After the head, the rest of the body is slowly touched, revealing to both the person being touched and the one touch-ing the complexity and vastness of their physical selves. In a variation of this touch experience, one member lies face up-ward with eyes closed and is touched by several others. Feel-ing more and more fingers exploring one's body can lead to some uneasiness at first, but if sufficient group rapport has developed this activity may become fairly reassuring. In an-other variation one member touches two others simultaneously. He might, for example, explore the heads of two other partici-pants, trying to understand and verbalize the differences he experiences.

Stretching is a good way to vary interactions that threaten to become sterile and fatiguing. Both elementary school classes and athletic events have stretch intermissions and encounter groups might follow their example with a few variations. Mem-bers may be urged to change from their sitting positions, stand up or lie down, and slowly stretch their muscles. A participant lying prone might slowly fully extend and reach with his left arm and right leg, then relax and try the same stretch with the other arm and leg. Others might try facial stretches: opening the mouth wide, extending the tongue, furrowing the brow, and otherwise limbering the face. Participants can also help each other stretch every muscle and limb from the top of the head to the fingers and on through the toes. Such cooperative stretching obviously helps enhance interaction and can be used, like touching, to add new dimensions to self-other aware-ness and deepen the group's psychological relationship.

Massage, in addition to all its other values, is also a body awareness technique. Members may rub each other's neck, back, and limbs and feel the muscles relaxing. The member being massaged can learn how his being responds to the touch of another. When it is his turn to massage someone else, he can appreciate how pleasurable it is to touch and how the skin and muscles of another are formed and respond. Generally the massage should be gentle, done through light clothing unless circumstances make bare skin appropriate. The objectives for both the person being rubbed and the massager should be pleasure, relaxation, body awareness, and emotional contact.

Lifting

Lifting exercises have received a great deal of publicity. Whenever one sees anything about encounter in any of the media, one is likely to see a group of people jointly lifting one member. Some group enthusiasts hail lifting as a uniquely unifying experience, but I am very doubtful that it has any special value other than being fairly dramatic. However, when circumstances warrant and members seem interested one might try lifting; it is a rather pleasant activity, giving a remarkable sense of freedom and lightness to the person being lifted.

One must be sure to lift properly to avoid injury to anyone. The member to be lifted lies face upward and is asked to relax and be passive. Members slowly lift and shake his limbs to induce a wavy feeling of passivity. When the supine individual is thoroughly relaxed and has his eyes closed, the group members kneel by his side and put their hands under him. One person holds the head, another is at the feet, and at least three others are along each side supporting legs, torso, and shoulders. If these eight encounter members are not particularly strong or in good shape, and/or the person to be lifted is quite heavy, the exercise should not be attempted; there should be absolutely no doubt that the safety and comfort of all are assured.

After their hands are firmly placed under the supine participant, the kneeling members slowly lift together, perhaps following one person's signals. When the supine person has been lifted to about knee height, members may pause as they stand up. Finally the person is brought to shoulder height and ultimately is held high above the others' heads. Some groups turn, or rock slowly and gently, when the full lift is reached. Finally the person is slowly lowered to the ground.

Every member should have a turn being lifted, though one or two may need some reassurance or even prefer not to participate. As in all body activities all objections must be honored, possibly discussed, and there must not be any attempt to force participation.

Looking and Seeing

Looking at ourselves in a mirror can be a surprisingly new educational experience if it has been preceded by some other seeing activities. Sometimes it is worthwhile to suggest a group stop talking for a while and use some other senses. Some sensitivity-type exercises may be tried. Participants might hold, touch, and study a rock or piece of wood. Or they might take a short walk with eyes closed, pausing every few steps to experience and possibly describe the new smells or sounds. The value of whatever sense activities are employed lies partly in the awareness but mainly in the pleasure they bring. After all, seeing, touching, and other sensual activities are among the most positive experiences in life. Enjoying their biological capacities increases the satisfaction encounter participants experience in each other, which may itself be sufficient justification for these exercises.

In addition to increasing joy, sensory exercises do sharpen perceptiveness. Doing looking exercises before looking at oneself in the mirror is often quite effective. When we have learned to see all the nuances in a rock we will see our faces in a totally different way. Perhaps now we will observe the delicately etched lines others have detected, which reveal our anxieties or perhaps our good humor. After members study their faces in a mirror to see what they reveal, they might try on new expressions, together with a partner. Members can try looking angry, jealous, morose, bored, or surprised, checking with each other and the mirror to see how effectively they assume the proper emotional mask. Partners might also try such games as communicating feelings through facial expressions.

The Meaning of Body Involvement

Only a few of the many, often ingenious body activities have been mentioned. In some groups members are asked to lie on the floor or crawl about to get a child's perspective. In others people struggle and grope their way in or out of a group in an attempt to simulate the feeling of breaking in or out socially. In still other groups members may slap, tap, or pinch each other; sensory isolation and deprivation trials may be attempted; throwing, catching, and blanket-bouncing and rolling may be carried out. These activities, if they are otherwise appropriate, may have value in simply helping the group feel more comfortable and intimate, contributing to the group rapport.

However good the experience has been physically, its worth should be discussed by the group. Bodies have probably acquired some new meaning for all. The physical tasks might have helped members feel better about themselves. The tasks may also have reducd guilt and increased pleasure in affectionate contact with others. Finally, most participants have probably recognized that exercises involving the whole being facilitate the total relationship. This is how one encounter member described a contact session:

> After about our fourth meeting we felt that things had slowed up between us. There was no one to guide us; it was the kind of group where we did pretty much what we wanted. . . . So someone had the idea of sitting in a circle on the floor . . . holding hands . . . then we moved very close and we touched . . . then we turned to each person next to us and we hugged . . . then we lay around and sort of stroked each other . . . and before you knew it we had spent the entire time in just physical things. . . . But the value of that experience was that it brought us together in a way that words could not do at that point. You need some physical demonstration of affection to really clinch it between people. . . .

Another encounter member described her touch experiences as primarily liberating. She had felt afraid of physical contact most of her mature life. But one of the things she learned in her group was that touch could be freely pleasurable.

> There's just nothing so human, and beautiful and good, as to be hugged and loved and patted. You feel the warmth of another person and their sincerity and I turn on to that. . . . It is sexual, I know that but it doesn't frighten me anymore. . . . I have rid myself of the attitude that any body pleasure, except what's supposed to happen between husband and wife in bed late at night, is wrong. . . . It's like Jilly was saying, there is no black and white but a whole range of colors in between with different degrees of body pleasure. And I feel that I am learning to work my way up through that whole color scheme and really am enjoying it for the first time. . . . I feel now I can understand others since now I understand my own body first. . . .

To recapitulate: body activities are usually worthwhile although they are not indispensable to encounter. Their advantages are multiple, ranging from relieving fatigue to increasing pleasure, overcoming barriers, and furthering the group's objectives. On the other hand, physical contact cannot be expected to do the work that only open and frank verbal communication can. For the same reason body experiences must be fully and carefully evaluated by the group, and the needs and inclinations of members must determine what (if any) physical exercises might be appropriate for them in their growth relationship.

Chapter 9

Learning Trust: The First Stage

Every encounter is different, just as each person who participates is distinct. Yet every group, unique though its situations and personalities may be, evolves through several identifiable stages. We cannot forecast in detail every sequence and outcome for every growth group. Each encounter is moved in somewhat different directions by the personal needs and special goals of its members. Further, the group as a whole often attains a momentum and spontaneity that in many ways exceed the contributions of the individual members. But my own experience and the wealth of information about group dynamics gathered by other psychologists allow me to outline what is likely to happen in any growth group.

Characterizing encounter (or the emergence of any other human relationship) in stages can become a sterile academic exercise. Interactions flow and recede. Explosive moments of revelation contrast with monotonous plateaus. Motivations and behaviors thread themselves through all sorts of early and later group and personal interactions in marvelously complex ways. Often what takes place at a fourth or fortieth encounter is so subtle or intricate that trying to recognize the stage of the relationship is virtually impossible. But however fluid, overlapping, and elusive each stage may be, it is worthwhile to attempt some differentiation of the growth experience.

Those who analyze the growth experience will learn that what happens is neither immediate nor magical. Meaningful interactions take time, endurance, and patience. Progress takes place slowly and fitfully. The first meeting or even the fifth may not seem very significant; but the group that persists, is expertly guided, and is beneficently motivated will certainly begin to find its experience rewarding by the fifteenth session. Members may not find personal changes obvious even after twenty meetings, but working through the growth stages during the last few meetings is likely to make them more and more aware of new potentials in themselves. In these last three chapters the stages of encounter will be described in the order in which their content is actually felt and experienced. A close look at each stage (and the techniques appropriate to each) will suggest what should or could occur; this may help direct members' expectations and effort.

What's a Nice Guy (or Girl) Like Me Doing in a Group Like This?

The most common reaction of encounter members at the beginning of the first meeting is suspicion and uncertainty. Certainly there is expectation and hopeful excitement, but beneath is the feeling confessed by one member at a second session: "What's a nice guy like me doing in a group like this?" The assumption he made—and most of us have similar thoughts—is that whatever our own eccentricities, we are fundamentally healthy human beings. When we look at our group for the first time, we think, "Some of those people sitting around over there certainly look weird." A thirty-three-year-old woman put it this way:

The most immediate feeling I had when I met the others

for the first time was, did I want to be identified together with people like that. Was I supposed to be like one of them? . . . Did I look, to some of them, the way they looked to me? After I thought about it a while I recognized that my real fear was almost opposite. I wanted to become part of this group and I was afraid that I would not become one of them. . . . I wanted to be liked and trusted by them and would they want me . . . did I have anything to say that would be good?

It is evident from this participant's description that the first group meeting presents every member a number of problems. Many are shocked at meeting their future group companions, for the implication is that all are similar; all are admitting weaknesses and imperfections and are openly asking for the care and assistance of others. Too, members are confronted with the dilemma of wanting to maintain their individuality yet wanting to change sufficiently to be accepted into a group. ("Will they like and accept me and value what I have to say? Can I become a complete part of their group and still not be swallowed by them and overwhelmed?")

Because of the strangeness of the situation and the doubts and uncertainties harbored by most members, first meetings are rarely very enlightening or productive. Confusion and frustration are natural and abundant. Whether or not a starter technique is used (chapter 4), there is bound to be much discussion at cross-purposes. Carrie may think she has said something very interesting and is anticipating a response; but Wade, who talks next, has obviously been waiting his turn to say his own piece and completely ignores Carrie's comments. Someone mentions the seating arrangement, and to half the members' utter boredom a prolonged discussion ensues among four participants about seats and pillows and chairs. Everyone's having had a chance to talk and no one's becoming particularly upset are about the only achievements that can reasonably be expected. If all the members leave after the first meeting feeling a little more comfortable, the objective of the introductory session has been attained.

Removing the Self

Once the confused chatter, polite surface interaction, and initial uneasiness of the first meeting or two have been overcome, members start significant talk about themselves. But the descriptions are likely to be hesitant, often contradictory, and above all remote. We are not yet sure just how much we can trust the others and are exploring the limits very carefully. Consequently whatever aspects of the self are talked about are often put in the past or made to seem very distant.

> Well I had a real problem with authority figures when I was a kid. I could never get along with teachers. I could never take being bossed around. . . . That was the kind of character I was then . . . always getting into an argument with my boss or whatever. . . . I had six different jobs the first year I got out of the Army. I was some kid then. . . . Now I'm twenty-five . . . I think I'm different. Maybe.

The preceding description, like many early encounter self-revelations, is not only made to seem distant; the feelings are also pictured as being unacceptable. Typically much of what is revealed about the self in the early stage of encounter is fairly negative. Member after member recalls his lack of success, displeasure with himself, and general unhappiness. Participants do this not only to unburden and seek counsel but also because they are half-consciously testing their group. They reveal a little they believe is not very commendable in order to see how it sits with the others. If what they say seems acceptable, if they are still liked by the group, then perhaps they can hazard telling even more. If the other participants disapprove, the confider will still be fairly safe because he has been careful to make his negative personal description appear to be about a self that existed in the remote past.

Incidentally, it should be apparent now why the kind of verbal encouragement and acceptance discussed in chapter 5, "Listening and Talking," is so critical. If others voice disapproval of a member's remote and vaguely self-disparaging revelation, they silence him. In telling the group negative things about himself the member is actually looking for acceptance and encouragement ("Can you still like me when you learn what I have done?"). If others indicate they still value him, the member can move forward. But if they make negative judgments they end his growth.

The following is an excellent example of an early self-description which is self-critical and is made to seem remote. At a number of points the narrative might have ended, but since the participants indicated their acceptance of Vic, the speaker, he was encouraged to continue.

Vic: If you want to talk about having had trouble, I have had a little bit . . . though it's over now, I guess. Anyway, I come from a small town in the South and I started smoking pot when I was in about tenth grade. And out of about 500 people in the school there were only three or four of us who were getting stoned and naturally we were either ostracized from the rest of the people or we separated ourselves from the whole social atmosphere of the school. And because it was so far from the city I really had no conception of what was going on in the city. A lot of people in the city were getting stoned in tenth grade, but my friends and myself considered ourselves much more progressive, much more advanced for our age, than everyone else in the world. . . .

Bella: You felt ahead of the rest.

Vic: Yeah, and then I came to the city and you know it was very shocking, I mean I was just a kid then, 'cause the first day I was there some guy that my friends at home had told me to go see, he was really into dope. . . . I started turning in that direction 'cause I'd gone through three or four years and I'd been a total nonconformist. I mean then if it was nonconformist, I wanted it.

Sol: You were very nonconformist then. That was all then that seemed important to you.

Vic: Yeah, that was then, that was my past (*laughs*) . . . but now (*pause*) . . . well, let me tell you that, and this is really the main part of my story, I feel like this is true confessions (*laughs*). . . . Well, anyway, in the city I got into some really heavy type criminal activities, directed towards dope and I guess directed towards society in general. After about a year of all this I got picked up and the police were threatening me with about ten or fifteen charges . . . a whole bunch of felonies. But I didn't think they really had anything on me that they could prove but I just decided to get out of there. I guess that arrest just sort of shook me out of the whole thing and I just sort of gave up and ran. I went back home and decided to forget about it all. Maybe that would be that and it would be over. Anyway a few days later I was driving around, outside my town, it was hot, and I was driving along and all of a sudden this car keeps trying to pull me over, get next to me. And then next thing, it was like these three freaks, they all had long hair, and I looked over and the guy on the passenger side was combing his hair (*laughs*), and next thing he points a gun at me. I thought I was being ripped off or something, 'cause like they all had long hair. I thought I was being ripped off. . . . I finally pulled over and I realized they were police from the city who had come all the way to my town to find me. I didn't realize how serious some of the things I had gotten into were, until that time. And even when this started happening I was joking about it. I was taken back to the city and I was questioned about ten hours straight about all these things and even then I was cocky about it. . . . Next day I was in court and my sister was there, she had sort of almost raised me, and there all of a sudden I just started to come down. That was bad.

Liz: You really had some experience. . . . I mean it's just like something you see on TV. . . . And you seem to have done so well with all those frightening things happening.

Vic: Well thank you, but I guess it sounds bad when you tell it, but, no, it wasn't so much. Even what we had done was almost more like a practical joke. Like the main charge was that we had broken into a hospital and stolen drugs. But that wasn't that much. This other guy and I we dressed up as security men, or guards. The other guy's brother worked as a security guard and we swiped some of his uniforms and drove to this big hospital in the city, very late at night. We just wandered in, walked around very cocky, everybody just thought we were new guards or something. . . . Anyway we just took whatever we could lay our hands on. We took all sorts of pills from different nursing stations and finally when we found the pharmacy we busted in. We got thousands of barbiturates and tranquilizers and everything else. . . . Anyway some of the people we sold to got busted and they ratted on us to try to get themselves a good deal. So when they came to my town they searched all over and they found a lot of these pills and stuff. . . .

Sol: I feel bad, Vic. This is something that sounds very serious, much more than a practical joke, and I'm wondering how you handled it psychologically. You seem to have been able to remove yourself from this experience. . . .

Vic: Well, it wasn't that bad for me but my friend, the one who turned me on to this (*laughs*), I guess you could say it was very bad for him.

Liz: He took it very badly.

Vic: You could say that (*laughs*); he was pulled over in his car in a parking lot in a shopping center outside the city, right off the speedway. He was sitting in his car with this other guy making a deal and they saw this cop's car coming over. My friend had all this dope so he figured he better get out of there and he had a very fast car, a Corvette, so he pulled away and these cops ran back to their car and they must have radioed. They put up roadblocks, everything, and finally they caught up with the car in traffic . . . and they fired right into the car and the one guy was shot through his neck and his thigh and my friend was shot right in the head and killed. . . .

Sol: Good God! And you described this all as if it were a big joke.

Vic: Well, I don't mean to, it's just the way it came out I guess.

Liz: What I think Vic is trying to do, Sol, and it is not easy, is talk about himself and he did have a bad experience, but it is not easy to talk about and that is why it may come out like that. He is being more courageous than many of us that haven't really even tried to say anything about ourselves yet, no matter how it comes out.

Unlike Sol, Liz understood why Vic told his story with an affected air of indifference. Vic's group was at the very beginning of encounter. Members who spoke up needed to test the others and simultaneously protect themselves. Vic wanted the affection and support of the rest and he was asking to be liked at his worst, for then he could be more sure his inclusion in the group was genuine.

Slowly and Carefully

At the beginning of encounter most individuals venture some tentative, remote-sounding, and often negative self-descriptions. But not all group members are even this daring. One or two members may say little or nothing about themselves till almost the last meetings. During most sessions they may have had serious doubts about their acceptability, felt guilty about revealing anything, or simply not known how to begin. Whatever their reasons they tend to sit quietly, supportive of others but not involving themselves. Obviously the group must not pressure such people to live up to their own theoretical stage of interaction ("We're all at the 'remote self-description' stage, why aren't you"). Not everyone will always be at the same level or stage of progress. Some members lag behind, some surge forward, and this discrepancy and overlap may be what gives good groups much of their vitality.

Very similar to the members who remain relatively quiet are those who actually resist the self-descriptions of others. Partly to protect themselves, they try to persuade others to be less open. Often they particularly resist hearing negative self-descriptions. They want to maintain a public impression of polite friendliness and not be forced to deepen relationships. Hearing another talk about his faults and flaws forces members to make basic decisions about trust and acceptance which are easier to avoid. Encounter would be much easier if instead of talking about substance, members maintained their discretion, encouraged one another politely, and rescued their facade.

Ella: I'm afraid of my parents too, I guess especially my father. It's usually all right when he and my mother are hitting it off but when there is any tension we all suffer. He gets jealous and mean and he is threatening. . . . I'm nineteen and yet I'm afraid of him when I go home and it's crazy. . . . I think I have an extra problem with him and me, because I think he has feelings he is ashamed of. He'll drink, and he drinks a lot sometimes, and then sometimes he's tried to come over to me and be all sweet and he'll try to reach out like to hold me and everything, and. . . .

Casey: Are you sure you want to talk about that, Ella? How would your father feel if he knew you were talking about him, personally, in front of so many others? I thought we were here to talk about how we could progress ourselves . . . not talk so much about others. . . .

Garth: Let her talk, it's her right and I think she is showing us how to really let ourselves go. . . . We all got to learn to be more open.

Kimble: Casey feels that this might be too much to talk about now. At least that's the feeling I get.

Casey: Well thank you all (*laughter*), no, really I thought maybe it might make some of us uncomfortable to hear so much right at the start. . . . I guess that maybe I was judging from myself.

All of us wear masks. Our public selves facilitate many ordinary everyday functions and usually become so much a part of us that they are not easy to drop. Casey was not yet ready to put his facade aside, as evidenced by his concern when another threatened to do so. It is likely he did not yet want to know Ella more than superficially or reach decisions about what she was saying. (But as his last statement reveals, unlike many participants who object to the self-revealing descriptions of others, Casey was at least partly aware of the sources of his hesitation.)

The fact that some members may remain silent for relatively long periods or otherwise actively resist self-revelation in others or themselves is not cause for disapproval. All honest hesitations, whatever form they take during initial encounter, must be respected. Obscuring ourselves by making our history seem distant (as Vic did) and cautioning another to be less open (as Casey did) are some of the ways in which nearly all of us indicate anxiety about a new situation. Group members' well-being demands that they move ahead very tentatively and slowly. Encounter cannot and should not be rushed or condensed, just as, say, courtship cannot be demanded or forced. The building of acceptance, fidelity, openness, and affection is a very slow, gradual, and delicate process.

I feel strongly enough about the necessity for growth's being gradual that I not only caution against rushing but affirmatively counsel going slowly and carefully. Thus it may sometimes be necessary to hold back a member who seems to be struggling into something neither he nor the group is ready for. Often a few encounter members have read, heard, or seen so much about groups that they are bursting to "get started." They want to pour everything out instantly and expect others to do the same. The guide or another member who senses that someone is prematurely revealing too much about himself may want to gently discourage a member from going further.

Felix: I'm personally turned off by discussions about sex. I don't like physical sex, in the movies or books. . . . I think love is very beautiful. Love is for everything in the world. . . . I don't see why you always have to make love physical. I love all creatures. I like pets, I like people, men and women. No, I love woman, I love man, there are many people I love. I don't think you have to call someone deviant or anything if you love everyone or even if the one you love is also a man, or a woman if you are a woman.

Cindy: Love is love, whether for a man or woman.

Felix: Yes and I want to say just how I really feel about this, but it isn't easy for me, people do not always understand.

Curtis: Then, I guess you might suppose, it might be better to wait awhile, till we all understand everything and each other a lot better. . . . Maybe we should understand each other more first.

Tod: Yes, I think so. I don't know whether we're ready or I am. Maybe someone else might like to talk about how they feel about love and emotion.

In this discussion Curtis senses that Felix might reveal some very deep feelings about his own different sexuality that might make other members uncomfortable. In turn this might make Felix feel rejected and discourage his further participation in the group. In short, during the first few hours of encounter members need to hold back, opening up only a little. They should go very slowly and carefully. Growth encounter should not be turned into a stress experience. Members are not brought together to shout out everything they know about themselves in dramatic but futile confrontations. There is undoubtedly entertainment and histrionic value in people's being pressured into supposedly deep confessions, but whatever evidence we have about the worth of such experience tells us it is of little lasting benefit. The milieu in which maximum growth does occur is one characterized by gentility, warmth, acceptance, and patience.

Feedback

As meeting follows meeting members become more and more comfortable with one another. Many of their early doubts and conflicts are resolved, and they try increasingly to talk about themselves as they really are, here and now (chapter 10). One critical sign that differentiates the early uncertainty of encounter from the stage of increasing trust is that members begin to comment understandingly on one another's narratives. Sometimes as early as the first or second session, but commonly considerably later, members focus upon one another so effectively that they begin really to understand what is happening in one another's lives. Their responsive comments demonstrate the depth with which they perceive one another's motives and behavior. They are beginning to become aware of the real self behind the other's facade.

Mitchell: I don't like being put upon, either. It is natural for a man to want to lead. I was telling Sylvia that she ought to listen more to what I say and then she won't be confused. She has no self-confidence but I do. I have a responsibility for over 200 kids and I know how to take responsibility, I know how to be a leader and I exercise that right. When you are in charge of so many people, like that, then you just develop the qualities it takes, or you get on out.

Lloyd: You feel that you are a natural born leader and know how to take responsibility.

Mitchell: Right. But you got to have those qualities, you can't learn them.

Chris: Forgive me, but I don't see what Mitchell is saying, the way you do, Lloyd. I'm just wondering, Mitch, since you've said a lot about this leadership lately, if you might not really have some doubts about yourself like that; uh, I kind of feel you are putting forth this picture of yourself more and more tentatively . . . that is, I can feel your uncertainty here, about whether you really are the way you like to present yourself.

The kind of sensitive and corrective statement made by Chris is often called *feedback*. Feedback, a response to another or another's comment, may be a reflection, restatement, or less often a question or contradiction. More important than the form feedback takes is its content. Some individuals with other supposedly encounter-type experience seem to believe that feedback must be brutally frank comment or another's personality or likeability. They believe feedback statements resemble these:

I don't like the way you look at me, Clem. In fact there is very little about you that I do like. You come across to me like a cowardly dog, always barking with a bright yellow streak up your back.

You're very lazy. That's your problem. You are fat, slovenly, ill-organized, and downright lazy. You don't have any other problem but laziness. The other thing about your personality is that you're gullible. You'll believe anything anyone tells you.

Why do you hand us all that bull, Jay. You're not as cool as you think. Always agreeing with everybody, being so nice and loving. You are really an angry and aggressive nut, don't kid us. That's how we all see you. You can't fake us out.

Feedback that is helpful and constructive is *not* a statement of affection or disaffection; neither is it a verbal attack. Feedback is essentially a *corrective* comment on another's self-perception or insight. Its purpose is to let another in on our understanding so that he can gauge himself more realistically. Chris helped Mitchell comprehend what might have motivated his continual talk about leadership. She perceived his inner doubts and let him share her views. By opening herself honestly, she helped Mitchell correct his self-perception.

Feedback statements may also help correct psychological insights. A participant may believe that he understands some aspect of himself, yet his view may be shortsighted.

Jake: I know I have a problem relating with mature women but it's something I can't help. My mother always frightened me and I've been scared, you might say, of women my age or older, all my life. It's one of those scars you bear from childhood.

Murray: Well, Jake, I would have agreed with you till just about a couple of sessions ago. When you were talking about how you had a need to be intellectually superior, to be the experienced person in any relationship. I wonder now if that couldn't have something to do with why you married these ultra young girls twice in your life. Could it be that you feel uncomfortable with older women because they might know as much as you, and, you know, be your equal in intelligence and experience?

Feedback is not always simply a corrective comment, in the sense of correcting some error. Feedback may have a very positive flavor, being also a statement about motivation or insight that is beneficent and rewarding. Such reactive comments may be a statement of approval or an underlining of an asset that another has only partially glimpsed. The following are examples of positive feedback.

When you told us about your art, Alma, I was struck by how beautifully you used words to describe your feeling. You painted a picture with the words you used . . . you just seemed to be able to breathe a new life into sentences. . . . I think that's one reason I've begun to feel so close to you . . . you make things so alive.

Maybe you aren't optimistic enough. I for one see you just like you were hoping. I don't think you're stuffy or phony and I wouldn't worry about it anymore. You come across a very solid citizen, very together. And I mean this in the most positive way, I mean you literally radiate being solid, like any one of us could rely on you completely. And I think that most of us don't just respect you, we really have developed very deep liking for you. I know I have.

Both negative and positive feedback appear to emerge as the group members overcome their initial uncertainty and warm up to one another and their task. At the same time, once participants do begin reacting to one another, the growth of trust is accelerated. Now people really begin to believe that someone else is listening and wants very much to help. The group that rushes into feedback in a futile attempt to speed things up is likely only to stir up acrimony and debate. Telling a man that he is fearful of close relationships or is too insensitive, or letting a woman know she is negativistic and hostile, is telling a person something that is not easily accepted. When such feedback statements come too early, before the group has developed at least a minimum of trust and mutual affection, the end result is often a breakup. Some members drop out of the group, and the few participants left may end as a debating society.

I have participated in so-called marathon encounter situations in which, over the course of ten or twenty hours, everything that might happen slowly as the months go by was supposed to take place in a day or two. There were games and exercises to allegedly bring about instant confidence, openness, and trust. Members were coerced into telling every last intimacy about themselves and persuaded to reveal every reaction they had about each other within a few hours after they were first introduced. Frequently a great deal of tension, crying, and screaming occurred and was encouraged. Apparently some believe these experiences worthwhile. Some people with no other access to an innovative experience may be helped by such a group situation. But I suspect that, just as it has taken twenty or forty or more years of learning and experience to make a person what he is today, it will take at least a few months of group interaction to make him a little different tomorrow. Change takes time; evolution is a gradual, incremental process—that is why I repeatedly emphasize patience and going slowly.

Trust

As the encounter continues so many things happen simultaneously that it is difficult to know when one stage ends and another begins. After six to twelve meetings, it is usually evident to all that their early awkwardness and uncertainty is largely a thing of the past. Nearly everyone has talked about himself a good deal and discussed both his past and future with decreasing reserve. Members are talking fairly freely, and attempts to make their self-descriptions seem remote are diminishing noticeably. At the same time participants have begun to feel sufficiently comfortable and sure of one another that they are risking comments about mutual self-perceptions and insights. Given this situation, conditions are right for the emergence of the next stage of encounter. People are fully ready to talk about themselves directly. They are going to drop their facade, take off their mask, dismantle some of their defenses, and be themselves. They have learned trust.

Chapter 10

Self-Discovery: The Middle Stage

During the middle of encounter, the self comes into focus. Members become aware of their inner being and strive to probe the depths of their personality. They want to know who they are and what they can do. These new urges can often be sensed as a restlessness in the group. At the beginning of the encounter, the participants also manifested their apprehension; the novelty of the situation in which they found themselves made them feel strange and uneasy. Now that the group is comfortable, a new disquiet can be perceived. Members are impatient or seem tense with expectation. Relating remote events or giving self-descriptions that are distant and intellectualized is no longer acceptable. Everyone is anxious to go deeper, to intensify relationships and move forward.

When trust has developed in the growth group, participants may literally demand that polite facades be dropped—that efforts to mislead others or delude oneself cease. As one member put it, "I think the time is ripe to stop the nice guy act and be ourselves. Who are we fooling? We know we've only been putting our best foot forward so far." The demand for honesty, at the middle stage of encounter, results in people's becoming more open, telling one another frankly what they think and feel. Stripped of a good many defenses and increasingly mutually dependent, people move toward a greater personal commitment; put another way: the encounter participants are moving closer to revealing themselves as they really are. The almost universal feeling of trust has made it possible for real people to begin talking.

The Apparent Self

We are all many selves. Most obvious is the self presented to the world at large. More likely than not, we try to convey an image of competence, stability, and maturity. Yet we are not entirely fooled by what we project, for we have some realistic ideas about our own qualities. We may try to look assured but know we actually feel intimidated. We may succeed in convincing others we are self-possessed when in actuality we may be a bundle of shattering fears. In addition to realistic self-evaluations, we are likely to have highly idealized self-conceptions. We may feel insignificant but visualize ourselves famous and powerful. The self-picture we present is only a small and often highly deceptive part of the total self we actually are.

Not only are we all multiple selves, but much of what we perceive to be ourselves often changes before our eyes. Many of our traits are highly variable and depend upon the people we are with and the situations we are in. ("I don't know who I am; for one crowd I'm a wallflower and for another the life of the party. I don't know if either or neither is me.")

Add to all this complexity in defining the self the fact that much of what we are is repressed. All sorts of motives and behaviors are blocked out, shoved aside and not recognized. A great many affectional, sexual, and other potent strivings are likely to have been prohibited, perhaps even punished, since earliest childhood and are consequently no longer accepted. Little wonder that many are confused and at a loss to define who they are. They catch only fragmentary glimpses of their hidden selves and cannot differentiate the mask they wear from traits that are deeper or circumstantial.

We can start finding out who we really are by determining what others think of us. Someone else who is fairly astute and objective may learn a great deal about us which they can share. Most people have already found out they can not depend upon their close friends or relatives to help them gain self-understanding. What a spouse, parent, or other personally involved individual says about our character is quite likely to be highly biased. When we hear ourselves described as stubborn, energetic, or callous by someone close we suspect, often correctly, that this is a highly flawed perception serving the speaker's own interest. But in encounter people have an unparalleled opportunity to hear who they are. Now they are surrounded by people who are sensitive and caring, and whose perception is just about as unbiased as they are likely ever to find.

During the middle stage of encounter, members begin to comment upon one another's insight and perception. In the preceding section (chapter 9, "Learning Trust") I called this process *feedback*. Once begun, this kind of commentary alerts all to the possibility that they may now say candidly how they see others. People are talking openly, responding to one another's insights, and now perhaps they will react to one another's self-perception. When the group become aware of the possibilities of self-discovery they begin to ask questions about themselves. In contrast to the opening phases of encounter, when everyone wore the mask of amicability and cooperativeness, participants now reveal their self-doubts and confusion. Their questions reveal they are not the cool, collected persons they once appeared to be. ("I don't know why I get only so far in any relationship, I think of myself as very loving, but tell me why things always end so badly." "Who am I and just what are my capabilities? Am I really poetic? Do I really see creatively or am I just on an ego-trip?")

Group members not only ask questions about themselves

but often volunteer comments about the self they perceive in others. The people in the group have been working together long enough and have developed sufficient rapport that they know they can correct another's self-perception without hurting him. An appropriate comment made at just the right time will be not only accepted but valued.

Olga: I wonder if you've ever thought, Melanie, that you might be a little selfish. Maybe that's why you said you wouldn't want Paul's responsibilities.

Melanie: You seem to see me as selfish. That is, you feel that's a quality in me I'm not aware of.

Olga: It could be. I'm not sure yet. Maybe the word I want is something like hoarding or guarding. You seem to want to keep things in, not to let your affections out. You almost seem to be afraid of liking someone. Loving even. . . .

Melanie: You could be right. It's not selfish. Maybe scared to love or give. I want to think about it. It's heavy. Maybe that's why I reacted so to Paul.

Paul: I had some of the same feeling [Melanie] as Olga did. But I didn't know if I could put into words like Olga did. I didn't know if you were ready [Melanie]. I think you are.

Melanie: I don't know I am. But I'm thinking . . . I can think of other things that might fit in with what you said.

Corrective statements on another's self-perception are not a casual "shoot the breeze" affair. Even when the comment is perfectly timed and cordially received such corrections are weighty matters. Each person in the group is fascinated to hear what others think of him. This is the kind of reward that members have looked forward to. They have been awaiting the moment when their group feels close enough for each to let everyone else in on his perceptions. But no matter how rewarding it may be to reach the level of intimacy at which we trust what another says about us, it is frightening to see what we are like in another's eyes.

Growth group members recognize the ambivalence of feeling that surrounds feedback about another's self-perception. They know they themselves can be hurt by having some of their pretensions exposed and defenses dismantled. Typically, as a result of this sensitivity, and often without any formal caution, participants make feedback comments about another's self with care and affection. They want to help the other understand himself, and the more their vision seems to contrast with appearance the more hesitant and gentle they become. Often too, partially as a defensive maneuver, the comments are made with humor, for laughing together at their own and others' foibles makes relatively difficult statements easier to digest.

Connie: I have the feeling, and it's maybe best described as a suspicion, Joyce, that maybe you don't really understand what your son is trying to tell you. His communication might not be reaching you, I think. I'm trying to say this in the most positive way, but I wonder if this is not the real failure on your part.

Trish: Can I interrupt a moment, since I don't think I agree with you, Connie. Connie, I was wondering about how you feel about what you said to Joyce. Do you have the feeling that you are really helping her? Like do you think you are being considerate of where she is at?

Connie: I think so. I think I'm being helpful and considerate. I gave it a lot of thought.

Quentin: What I suspect Trish is driving at, correct me if I am wrong, is that you [Connie] have this idea about yourself. You see yourself as very understanding and helpful. But you don't come across like that to some of us.

Connie: I feel altruistic and unselfish and I feel like I am trying to help but you don't all see me that way.

Trish: Hm hm. Quentin is right. He's also being very direct like he is (*laughter*). I feel you really try to be helpful and you are natively kind. But there's something else mixed in with you when you are considerate. And you are considerate, I have no doubts about that (*others agree*). But you also mix in some take-charge sort of attitudes. You seem to want to take over from Joyce or anybody in that situation.

Quentin: I wouldn't be able to say it as well as Trish but that's how I feel. I think you really are good but you get that take-charge idea mixed in and then you lose something valuable.

Connie: You see me as watering down my good intentions. Trying to grab control at the same time.

Trish: I don't know if it is that strong, but it's like that.

Verbal abuse, attack, and malevolent comments concerning another's self-perception are rarely productive and have no place in growth encounter. Members of a group that has worked slowly and patiently to reach a good interaction are not likely to attack one another. But the group that is misdirected and harried is likely to be very abusive and may well be harmful before it ultimately dissolves. Someone caught in this kind of unhappy group situation should leave. In the few instances in which an otherwise good encounter results in abusive comment, such remarks are usually best handled by reflection (though under some circumstances, some other growth techniques mentioned previously might be applicable).

Reflective comments are most in order since malevolence is triggered primarily by distress. The reflection thus not only suggests the inappropriateness of the unfortunate response but also offers an insight that may help relieve the source of discomfort.

Aaron: You want to know what we think of you. Well I'll tell you. You are what I call a secret S.O.B. You're mean, thick-headed, and sly to boot. . . .

Ariel: You seem quite upset, Aaron. . . .

Aaron: I'm not upset, I'm mad. No one can say the kind of thing Scott is saying, so nice and friendly on the outside, without being a secret louse inside.

Ariel: You're angry then because you feel Scott is a secret louse, or whatever, inside.

Aaron: Well maybe I'm more mad than I should be. It may

not be what you said before, Scott. Maybe it's me, I don't know.

Skip: Drop dead, both of you! You're sluts, that's what you are! Leave me alone, you're no good. Just no good.

Harvey: Wow, I mean you are upset. I can sympathize with you. I know you don't dig their life but wow, why did you have to come on like that? What's eating you? You've got to have something heavy on your mind.

Skip: I got on my mind, as you say, the fact that you are all sitting here listening and shaking your head and everything is all right, and I am saying it is not. They are not creative and loving. Bull. There is still a right and a wrong and ways of doing things that are proper. . . .

Harvey: So you feel you should let us all know what they are doing is not proper. . . .

Skip: I mean someone has got to raise his voice once in a while and bring us all back to reality.

Mickey: Let me just start on another track for a moment; [Skip] you're telling us, you hate Midge and Harriet because of what they've been saying. . . .

Skip: No, I'm not telling you anything about them. . . . I'm lost . . . I'm sorry. I lost my head. I don't hate you [Midge and Harriet]. . . . I hate myself . . . I'm intolerant, I suppose like Jackie said before. I guess that and what Midge said, with Harriet. I didn't want to hear any more.

Learning how they appear to others enables encounter members to probe more deeply within, to understand themselves. Now everyone can learn just who everyone else is. Each member can know the others both as they appear on the surface and, to a large extent, as they are underneath. They need no longer hide themselves; they can express fully all their longings and experiences.

Self-Expression

Following closely (if not simultaneous with) solicitation

and commentary on members' self-perception is increasingly meaningful self-expression. Members have been told how they seem to others, and to the relief of all the results have not been catastrophic. Participants are now emboldened to reveal even more potent material. Whatever thoughts or recollections come to the fore are verbalized or otherwise introduced to the group. Members feel almost compelled to tell all, to be uninhibited, to state who they are and how they feel here and now. There is often almost a palpable sense of gratification now that most are responding with candor and immediacy. There is a recognition that something is being learned for the future—that being themselves here in the group, right now, will liberate and strengthen them for much of what may happen later, outside the group.

Often what starts as a not too provocative commentary about another's self-perception leads to very deep and significant self-expression. Sometimes a member strikes just the right chord in another and presents a magnificent opportunity for the other to "ventilate" and be himself.

Phil: I know why you say that, Elsa, and it's because you feel so secure. Being a doctor's wife and looked up to, you radiate security but I sometimes wonder how you really feel inside. Sometimes you seem almost timid, I don't know, frightened maybe.

Elsa: I seem to look scared to you, and not as secure as I look on the outside.

Phil: It's just a feeling I get. Like now, this evening, I'm wondering what might have happened to you today. You seem to want to radiate confidence, but you also seem tense. I mean you were right what you said. But you still seem hurt.

Elsa: You're very perceptive. I don't know if it's all that important though. I may not be as secure as I seem, I guess. Anyway I was a little shaken today. I had a long talk with my husband this afternoon. . . . He and I were talking about his being a doctor. And he was telling me, again, how important his work is . . . how much he is needed. That he likes to feel how he touches the lives of so many people in ways that are more than just being a doctor to their bodies. And we got into quite a heated discussion I suppose. . . . I started getting upset. I started in criticizing him for playing God, like doctors do, and wanting to run other people's lives. *(Elsa is becoming emotional as she tells her story.)* The more I criticized him the more upset I got, it was more almost as if he didn't even listen to me. He wasn't even seeing what he was doing to me. And we were supposed to be so happily married and good together. And so often I feel so alone and so frightened. . . . And he kept telling me how he liked to touch the lives of others. And I got louder and louder and said, "Touch, touch," and I yelled and I screamed and I said "Touch me, oh God, touch me!" *(Elsa pauses. She is crying and others seem deeply moved.)* My God. I need to be loved.

Certainly self-expression, like most of what occurs in encounter, can go astray. Sometimes uninhibited comments become increasingly negative and destructive. This may happen in even the best groups, for a little negative feeling is typical. One individual may attack another as being "tough" or "egotistical" or "exploiting the women in this group." Occasionally too the guide is attacked as too "bossy" or, conversely, "sitting back and not helping us a damn."

In productive group situations aggressive comments do not escalate and are soon replaced by more positive expression. Often these verbal attacks are simply the way in which very doubting members test whether they are really accepted by the group or can say anything they choose without being ostracized. Whatever the motives for negative self-expression, and the feelings may be subtle and complex, when the whole group is otherwise purposefully directed towards growth the negativism is an ephemeral, rapidly passing phase. Thus it is best simply to accept such commentary without much fuss. If, on the other hand, the remarks seem disturbing, they might be carefully reflected, since pointing to the underlying feelings is often sufficient to clear the air. Handled in the same way as malevolent comments (discussed earlier in this chapter), self-expression that is abusive will not seriously interrupt a good growth group.

A fairly minor problem that may occur as self-expression increasingly characterizes the group is that a few members, over-enthusiastic, seem to get carried away. Enthralled by the notion of being themselves, of immediately saying whatever comes to mind, they determine henceforth to be totally genuine. Consequently they may startle the group with such comments as "I'm bored to tears with what's going on today" or "Your body excites me. Let's leave and make love." Such verbal intrusions, though abrupt, are usually quite benign and occasionally even worthwhile stimulants. More embarrassing are attempts by a few members to carry the spontaneity of honest self-expression into their jobs or homes. While receiving instructions from his boss one group member reported he said, "I could take your orders a lot better if you washed more often so you didn't smell so much." Another encounter participant told her sister-in-law, "If you peek into another one of my closets I'm going to shove you inside and lock the door."

Overdoing uninhibited self-expression is seldom a really serious impediment. But in the few instances in which encounter begins to be dominated by unrestrained talk and behavior the group interaction does suffer. Communication ceases, for instead of listening to one another and seeking to understand, members only react to their own internal cues. This is best remedied by redirecting everyone's attention to the main goal of the encounter. The ultimate purpose is growth, and self-expression is just a step along the way. Those too free on the job or elsewhere soon learn also that spontaneity is a powerful new skill. Like all potent abilities it must be shaped to meet the conditions in which we live and must be adapted to our larger goals.

The Self

Growth encounter is not depth psychoanalysis; consequently

the extent of self-revelation, though profound, is partial. During analysis—if it is of sufficient duration and expertly directed —essentially every feeling and motive, however repressed, becomes conscious. The analyzed patient is made totally aware, ultimately, of all his weaknesses and strengths, desires and aversions. During encounter the discovery of the self, the lifting of repression, is more limited. Participants uncover enough of their core characteristics to become more genuine beings. They are enabled to understand themselves and their needs far more fully than ever before. While growth members may not become conscious of every trait and drive, they develop sufficient insight and new behaviors to initiate their self-actualization.

Much of the understanding of the self occurs towards the end of encounter. The group has built mutual trust, explored one another's self-perception, and in this way helped each person understand himself better. There is no guarantee of an orderly progression; encounter moves largely in spurts and waves, from the building of trust through self-discovery to growth. But what is supposedly a third-stage development may happen at the fourth meeting. Alternatively, at the twentieth meeting some good group members may still be working on areas that others resolved during the fifth. Emotions and behaviors are not packaged in neat, tidy segments. The sequence of personal maturation is fluid, overlapping, and subtle.

Just as the stages of growth encounter are dynamic, the evolution of self is far from static. Serious self-realization typically takes quite a while to occur but may also happen fairly early. Usually the self that is revealed first is characterized by needs and longings once suppressed. Next, after participants have come to grips with these long-buried frustrations, they become aware of many of their assets. This sequence is not invariant; but to simplify discussion, this section deals with the unearthing of needs while chapter 11 treats the discovery of potential.

Encounter may not progress to the growth stage but may end instead with self-discovery. Depending upon the group and circumstances, the encounter may end appropriately when members just begin to come into contact with themselves.

Sometimes groups work extra slowly, so that after forty or even fifty meetings most members have just learned to shed many of their defenses and be more spontaneously themselves. This may be as much as some people desire or as is appropriate, and such an end to encounter can be fully satisfactory.

Despite all the variations in sequence and path shown by growth groups, a uniformly climactic point of encounter is reached as individuals become fully aware of themselves. When participants no longer come together dressed in the protective armor of social bluff and disguise, they are ready to come to grips with one another. They are ready to peer inside themselves and see the person who actually lives within the role they have created for consumption by others. Seeing and experiencing the self is usually a frightening, lonely awakening. Knowing themselves is described by most members in terms very similar to these:

> I don't feel too comfortable looking at myself. . . . I feel empty, scared. . . . I think most of all I feel alone. . . . I know who I am and you know who I am and we all know I'm not covering up anymore. . . . It makes me feel naked, empty . . . but most of all I feel like I am here all alone, unprotected.

The first reaction of most encounter members when they see themselves without their defensive armor is one of vulnerableness and isolation. They now experience fully the alienation and anxiety that their disguises had shielded them from. Of course such feelings of despair exist at many levels and in many degrees. For some participants coming to grips with themselves involves proportionately little stress or discomfort. But most who are taking the risk of being themselves—and it is a very considerable risk—require the group's warmest support and acceptance. There are few moments more thoroughly gratifying than when the growth participants, sensing an individual's torment at self-discovery, respond with a depth and wholesomeness reserved only for genuine encounter. The group expresses its deepest affection for the real self, flawed and imperfect as it may be, with an intensity it has never shown for the superficial front.

During the thirtieth group meeting Josh was sitting fairly quietly, seemingly withdrawn from the group. He had usually been fairly talkative and had been spontaneous and intuitive during the last few meetings. He seemed also to have increasing depth of understanding for the obstacles others faced as well as his own. Towards the end of this meeting, Josh had still said nothing at all and seemed to be even more depressed and withdrawn. Marina—apparently sensing his despair—went over, sat next to him, and held his hand. He looked at her and seemed very sad and distant. Then Josh turned towards her, placed his head on Marina's shoulder, and cried softly. Marina held him and the group gathered round quietly.

"Tell me why you are crying," Marina said. Josh replied that he felt no one cared about him but when she came over he was too overwhelmed to put his gratitude in words. Josh continued to reveal that the more he got to know himself the more he felt he was a "loner, and an oddity." No one could really care about him, and his life and marriage were just a front to keep up good appearances. He felt he wasn't even worth loving. He was too selfish for anyone to care about. Marina responded that she cared and she thought that others in the group did too. Several members spoke up declaring their sympathy and affection. A few people spoke about how they also felt unloved. Marina told how she had periods when she felt so alone and unacceptable she had thought about suicide. She said she had been drawn to Josh without much conscious direction. When she had noticed him withdrawing she felt an urge to touch him to help him share some of the misery she had felt herself.

Loneliness and feeling unloved, unworthy, and inadequate are discovered by nearly all encounter participants as they come into contact with themselves. Less often, probably because it is more vigorously repressed, sexual distress is uncovered. Occasionally the erotic needs are intense and unconventional. Members may unearth sensual motives that differ from those sanctioned by society. To their surprise, in harmonious and advanced groups such longings are fully accepted and the individual who becomes aware of his erotic requirements is warmly received because of his openness, trust, and progress. More often, however, the sexual longings that are uncovered are surprisingly modest, demonstrating only how severely restrained the growth participant had been.

> I'd like to tell something that happened to me, I think because of what I said last week. . . . [*May had previously described how she was superficially sexually liberal, seeing some adult movies, making jokes, etc., but somehow still believed sex was dirty. She had in fact become fairly vehement during the meeting, saying sex was disgusting but feeling horror at her attitude since she wanted very much to enjoy sex in a full physical way.*] I know I cried and ranted last time that I wanted to enjoy sex but I had such a terrible block. . . . Anyway maybe because I said it to you all and you were so good to me and I experienced it out in the open, maybe that got rid of my feelings. . . .
>
> Anyway this morning after the kids were off to school Rudy was taking a shower and I was just lazing in bed and he came in, in a cloud of steam all naked and honestly looked like a God to me. And I got so terribly excited, and I was so thrilled I could feel this way, and I looked so hungrily at him and then I said, 'Don't dress,' and he was so surprised, and I think almost shocked. But I felt so good and I was so glad. And I touched him and kissed him in ways I have never done before. . . . I was just being the animal me, and we both loved it and he went to work very late that morning. We just kept going. . . . I never felt so good . . . and free.

The frustrations that lie within every person are doubtless too numerous to count. Most people have been taught to submerge their sexual urges, deny their desire for warmth, and disregard feelings of loneliness. In the name of respectability, decency, or a false sense of adultness many people have cultivated a veneer so efficiently that any real feelings are experienced only as distant echoes. Small wonder that the discovery of the real self is always an emotional experience for members and the group. Individuals and the group are often moved both to tears and to expressions of joy as they experience their own selves and the group's affection in ways they never thought possible.

> When I discovered that I can be loved, am loved, for what I am, and not what I pretend to be, that for me is the most monumental discovery I have made in encounter, if not in my whole life.

There are many roads to self-discovery. Capable people have often uncovered their potential through art, writing, or other creative and psychological enterprise. But growth encounter is the only way in which individuals can be put in touch both with themselves and with other persons who are real. Even within the family people all too often experience simply the impersonal acting-out of the roles of parent, teenager, or spouse. I believe that growth encounter is a singularly productive way of dealing with the superficiality and alienation that typify so many of our day-to-day interactions. If growth groups did nothing more than permit people openly to experience each other's substantial presence and warmth, their existence would be sufficiently justified.

Chapter 11

The Growth Experience: The Final Stage

The purpose of growth encounter is to help people actualize themselves. Through the group experience participants are enabled to loosen repressive inhibitions and overcome psychological blocks so that they can grow again as human beings. Towards the end of encounter, growth is usually evident in at least two areas. First, members have an increased understanding of, and desire for, significant personal relations. They want honest, warm, and loving ties with other people. Second, growth participants uncover what is good and worthy within themselves and move ahead seeking creative change and innovation.

Feeling and Love

During the last stage of encounter nearly every group member recognizes new and pleasant sensations within himself. Through their dedicated help and affectionate concern, the people he has come to know so well and worked so intimately with have stimulated the warmest, most tender emotions. To employ a word that has become overused and misunderstood: growth encounter has revealed itself as a *love* experience. At this point one can certainly sense, almost see, the exchange of mutually good feeling in the group. Early in the meetings, when someone spoke nearly everyone at least paid close attention. But now, after twenty, thirty sessions or more, the entire group's tone, posture, and gesture show the most genuine interest, deepest concern, and affectionate support. Obviously, by the time encounter nears its end every member has become a cherished and valued link; each participant is connected with everyone else.

The positive and shared emotions that come about during the final meetings provide each member an opportunity to reeducate or actualize his own feelings. For some the amicability originating in the group provides, literally, the first opportunity they have ever had to interact unselfishly with affection. Quite a few otherwise intact people seem never to have had any relationship other than one based on manipulation, convenience, irritating dependence, or reciprocal antagonism. Other participants who have had emotional relationships but whose feelings have been distorted by misunderstanding, suspicion, and frustration find the warmth of the group a reeducation in love. They learn from their encounter to sort out their own needs, freeing themselves of deceptions in the process.

The focus on love and feeling that arises during the closing stage of encounter elicits discussion that varies immensely in insight and intensity. For nearly all participants there is an increase in both self-understanding and feeling, but expression of both is relatively sedate. A few participants, however, experience their new comprehension and emotion almost as a revelation. They are exuberant with joy, feeling that now at last a new part of themselves has become known. They like what they are, now, and want their growth to continue.

The following statement was made by a middle-aged man who could not recall ever before feeling any tender emotion similar to what he was then experiencing in the group. Quite far-reaching in his perception, this member was able to trace his inner sterility to his adolescent rebellion against his parents. Like many teenagers trying desperately to be free, he had rejected even the legitimate concern of his mother and father so vigorously that as an adult he still backed away from anyone who seemed the least affectionate.

> This is the first time in my life since I was a kid that I like being liked. I am really glad to feel that you like me. It is an experience I never had before and it has made this last two weeks just marvelous. . . . I feel like I'm floating . . . I walk around and I smile to myself. It feels so good. . . . You may wonder why I say that I have never really felt love. How could I marry and have children . . . well I never did. I did what was expected of me that's all. . . . I think Liza put her finger on my feeling last time. I was always the machismo male, independent and hard. I never got over the fifteen-year-old image of the cowboy. Strong, and not saying much and not having any feeling for anybody. That's how I dealt with my parents when I was fifteen and that's how I had been ever since.

Similar to the male encounter members who recognize their cultivated supermasculinity as a flight from feeling are the women and men who have come from parental backgrounds that almost literally denied affection. They are likely never to have had any warming emotional experience whatsoever, for their parents substituted duty and discipline.

> I don't think I ever knew what feeling for someone was all about. When my mother died I remember trying to look sad. At the funeral I remember wondering about what the others would think if I just chattered away like at any party but I didn't do it. I felt it my duty to look sad so I did what was expected but I didn't feel a thing. . . . But when Saul was going through his trouble . . . I wept. Last week I wept here, I cried at home, and I'm crying now. . . . I know (*laughs*) it's not for you, Saul. You're O.K. I cried because I was so happy to feel something. . . . Like I'm laughing now too . . . I'm feeling and it's so good. . . . My family was so cold and distant I never saw my mother and father kiss. My father made the

rules and we all carried them out. We did what was right and proper. We got a nickel when we did something extra hard, like shovel snow. But we were always formal, and distant and aloof. I don't remember ever being hugged. The only time I was ever kissed was when I was sick. I remember lying in bed and very feverish and my mother put her lips to my forehead. . . . My family wasn't cruel. They were stiff but they were courteous and my father was proud of trying to make us tough. He didn't want sentimentality . . . which is what he called it.

While many encounter members trace their affectional emptiness to their family and childhood, some recognize that they had a worthwhile emotional start but that their original good feelings have been subverted and diminished. Even when youngsters come from a fairly warm family milieu, once they have been exposed to and "educated" by our entertainment media their most delicate needs may become grossly distorted. They are mistaught by film, television, and other fiction-vending media that love is something they "fall' into or out of as if in some kind of magical whirl. Supposedly there is just one "right" person for each of them who combines all the sexual, financial, or status attractions each craves. Lest we doubt that such fiction has much influence on people, we must recall that more than one-third of all American marriages now fail. Talks with those in the growing legions of the separated, divorced, and disillusioned show that many have tried to base their intimate marital relationship on little else but the superficial and exploitative kinds of attractions they have seen portrayed in countless fictionalized romances.

Hugh: The thought I had after Matthew talked was that you don't *fall* in love. I'll tell you why I say that. Because up till now I had to meet a girl that turned me on, right then and there. She had to have something magical about her . . . it was mainly physical, I'll admit. I knew that much about myself. Like Laurie who just split. When I first saw her, she really turned me on, man, what a body. . . . But as I got to know her better, and because at the same time I was getting to know you all better, I came to realize that I really didn't have much in common with her. . . . Attractiveness is not the only important aspect of a female. I have come to realize that being a physically attractive female doesn't have to mean that the entire person is attractive. This change hasn't been drastic enough for me to say that when considering a girl for a date or something, appearance won't play a part, but on the other hand appearance won't be the determining factor.

Alex: I understand what you're saying, Hugh, and I have similar feelings. You don't fall in love based on some superficiality. It's that Hollywood thing, like you said [Matthew]. It had me convinced that I had to search the field. I was flitting from one to the next waiting for the magic spark to light my fire. . . . But then I came here and I met all you people and frankly none of you were like any of the people that I had ever thought I could feel love for. . . . But then something slowly happened. We got to know each other more and more and I found I was beginning to feel something happening between all of us. . . . I understand it now, this way. Love comes from a good relationship. It is not the start of a relationship, it's something that comes along the way. . . . You've got to give a relationship a chance. Lots and lots of time and then maybe love will develop or it won't.

The discovery of feeling in first encounters is possibly the most important part of the growth experience. For most group members, getting in touch with their own emotions—sorting out true feeling from deception—is the greatest reward of their encounter participation. I have witnessed the birth of many of these moving and penetrating emotional perceptions, of which two other fairly common examples follow.

A few participants become aware that the way in which their interaction with others in the group has slowly evolved can serve as a model for future relationships. (Alex, quoted previously, was struggling with this idea.) They notice that at first they felt uneasy with what seemed to be a group of not too compatible-appearing strangers, united only by a common interest in growth. Slowly however, and very tentatively, the uneasy mutual exploration gave way to accelerating concern, care, and support.

> I think love is just what happened here. Two people meet and get to know one another slowly and the more they give to each other the more they become united by affection. Like in this group . . . no one was saying love me. They were helping me . . . they wanted me to become more myself . . . not take from me. . . . That's what happens, or it should, when you come to love someone . . . you come together . . . helping each other and before you know it your feeling has grown and grown and you love them.

From their encounter experience many members learn that love is not instant and not a response to another's supposed enticements. Love is the result of a mutually satisfying and encouraging interaction. In the words of a particularly articulate encounter participant, growth group members often begin to comprehend and feel that "Love is the fruit of a relationship, not its seed."

One cannot discuss or approach love (or for that matter almost any positive feeling) in our society without raising questions about sex. People in encounter also have to deal with the often confused margins concerning love and sex. Of course, by the end of encounter members are fully aware (as they should have been since the first orientation—see chapter 1) that despite sensational misreporting, growth encounter is in no way a cover for sexual exploitation. Participants are not forced to be ascetics or to leave all erotic feelings at home; there is, after all, physical attraction during encounter. Yet during the life of the group each member learns to put his sexual needs aside. The result of this differentiation is not frustration, as some might expect, but rather a new understanding of the congruence of sexual and loving feelings.

I didn't know I could really deeply like someone, without sex. To me it used to be that if you were a woman and you wanted me to like you it had to be sex. And the opposite was true. I couldn't feel sex without really liking somebody. I had the whole thing all pushed together in my mind. . . . Sex and love are very compatible and great together, but they can also be different and apart and just as good.

The affections exchanged, combined with the erotic limits imposed on the group and the outside experiences discussed, enable many members to see love and sex in proper perspective for the first time. They come to understand that love and sex may be united, separate, or take any number of forms. In contrast to the traditional view that love must be sexual, encounter members learn from their own experience that much love is plainly nonphysical. They also come to understand that sex can be entirely free of love commitments. It is often alleged that love is necessary to sex, sex "without love" supposedly being deplorable if not entirely evil. But just as there can be deep and meaningful devotion without any sexual involvement, erotic experiences can be good and pleasurable in and of themselves. Sex can be a joy shared by friends or even casual acquaintances. When every person in an encounter has opened up and the fullness of his affectional as well as physical needs is seen by himself and the other group members, it becomes apparent that there are few if any absolute norms defining sexual pleasure among healthy, self-actualizing people. The spectrum of libidinous needs is very broad and contains diverse forms, any of which can be desirable and life-affirming growth experiences.

As each encounter member's capacity to feel—to experience love—comes alive, a few groups are nearly swept by a contagious euphoria. Everyone feels so intact, joy is palpable, and paradise seems almost around the corner. Occasionally some participants speak almost poetically, and many show deep emotion in their voice and bearing. Here is an excerpt from a powerful letter that captures some of the feeling present in the closing moments of many growth groups. This note was from a member who had been fairly quiet in meetings and chose writing, after the group had ended, to convey her feelings.

I came to encounter and I ended it a 32-year-old wife and mother of four children. But little else is still the same. . . . Religion: Yes, not alone Episcopalian, but all faiths. Before the group I had nothing but an ancient hand-me-down label. Now I have all, for I have learned something about myself and my feelings for others. If it were necessary to describe this as a religious philosophy I would say it in a phrase from the *Analects* [of Confucius], "I choose unity—all pervading."

I am content yet feel the need to learn more. This I accept as a natural duality, much like the universal dualities of life-death, good-evil, fertile-barren, right-left. My goal: to transmit love, yet not necessarily to receive it. This love does not need sexuality or reciprocity. Sexuality is good, with or without love, being loved is good, and I have these things. I want this special love to stand alone. Just pure gut love that requires only giving. This perhaps is the influence of Jesus, as he really was and not as he is made out to be by churches and clergy. Jesus spoke for love and joy and not for moralizing, judging others or persecuting them.

I have yet not learned to extend my love to all living creatures and things, but just as my group began awakening I have hope more lies ahead. I believe that man is an animal, yet unique for he is endowed with the ability to reason and to care. With these abilities comes an obligation to the rest of the universe, be it plant, animal, mankind, or resource. Only when man gives all these love can he succeed. If we give love only to bargain for its return we can never succeed. . . . Given the desperate and unseeing state of so many it may seem impossible but I believe now that gifted with reason and emotion mankind may yet choose love. I have only a small start and perhaps many others more, and still many more others, less. Yet still I have faith for each year adds a little. . . .

For me this group has been an encounter of love. It rekindled my long sleeping faith that all people want to give, to love, yet so often don't know, or have forgotten how. . . .

Creative Change

When the months have gone by and the conclusion of the encounter is near, most members try to mobilize their new feelings and insights in order to bring about changes in their lives. They attempt to translate their understanding into action. This is an important and commendable step. Talking about one's improved self is worthwhile; but the discovery of potential and emotion is far more valid when followed, wherever feasible, by new behavior. For example, a member who has perceived that he has always run from deepening emotional relationships now actively encourages a deep interaction. A participant who was once totally domineering now opens herself up, diligently listening to the needs and directions of others. A participant who has recognized the emptiness of the housewife role she has played so dutifully for years returns to school, educating herself for a totally new career.

Not all encounter members should alter their personality, job, location, or marriage. Radical changes especially, such as divorce or giving up a remunerative career, are usually ill-advised. A beginning encounter experience should not lead to drastic, irreversible life revisions. What should emerge from an elementary growth group experience is a sense of new direction. A willingness to slowly, carefully, and tentatively take some first small steps. Frequently it is up to the group to encourage new endeavor yet counsel caution. New ideas require nourishment, but they may also benefit from another's more dispassionate assessment of reality. Plans need the wisdom, support, compassion, and evaluation of the encounter, just as did the insight and awakened emotion that preceded the call to action.

Britt: I no longer feel my life is a mystery to me. It all falls into place. I have the feeling that for the first time I know where I am going. . . .

Mae: You do look so good. . . .

Britt: I'm leaving home, and I am going to school and I'm going to become not just something . . . but a person. . . . I told my husband that I want to be educated . . . to read and listen to people that know so much more . . . maybe they don't but I want a chance to find out . . . and he pooh-poohed it. Bull and all that. . . . But I feel firm and convinced. . . .

Dick: You seem to feel very good about knowing yourself and what you want. . . . I agree you would really flourish in that atmosphere. But I feel scared about your saying you're leaving home.

Kevin: I get a very good feeling from you . . . and about you. . . . But I get the same fear. . . . Do you feel you could start by going to college and staying home?

Sonny: I'm not sure. . . . I know in my own head I want to start living free, like I described, and Heidi is for it too, and I am, but I really wonder if you don't think it's wrong or too much. I mean I really want an answer. It is not the most conventional path. . . . A lot of people even would think we were maybe even crazy, I don't know.

Lonnie: Well count me in. You know where it's at. I'm all for it.

Karen: What I think you're asking for, Sonny, is, well, maybe social approval. You are kind of testing to see if it fits our view. Well I am not going to beat around the bush and I say directly, Yes. Go ahead. You are doing it slowly, carefully, I think.

Joseph: What I think Karen is saying is that we may not be typical, but who cares. I think you're right and go ahead and try. You're not making a snap decision. We've all thought together for a long time now.

Lonnie: What we are all saying, I think, is that we trust you. We trust you. We trust ourselves. We've gone through it together and it's good.

Which changes should be encouraged in a first encounter? My own general rule is that I support any ethical, humane change that is thought out, relatively gradual, and likely to be beneficial not only to the individual but possibly also to those with whom he interacts. I do not support change that is probably irreversible, uncreative, or possibly harmful. However, growth group members are not put in the position of judging continuously whether one or another individual should be encouraged. In the vast majority of instances, in good encounters that have evolved cooperatively through the final growth stage, nearly all changes taking place are creative and worthwhile. Whether the individual's new plans include business, art, travel, education, writing, communal living, a new life style, or significant modifications in relationships, if he and his group have gone through a mutually productive encounter the chances are excellent that his ideas are solid.

Growth that occurs in encounter need not be limited to a creative change in life circumstance. Through the intervention of the group, individuals may have seen their character clearly for the first time and consequently stand ready to change their usual behavior. Old outworn and dead-end habits and traits may be dropped and more useful behaviors substituted. Often a personality trait has persisted since childhood, and though the participant is now fully grown he acts in the old habitual childhood manner. Andrew, for instance, was able to trace the fact that he always seemed to be arguing with others to a negativism that had remained since infancy. Like many other children he originally began to say no to parents and older siblings to defend himself against an overbearing mother and older brother. Yet though he was now an adult he still said no or reacted negatively to almost any comment. The result was that he was nearly always disputing with someone.

> When I started watching myself, after we talked about it here, I was dumbfounded ... there was hardly anything anyone ever said that I didn't say no or disagree. Like you would say, "I think it's going to rain," and my automatic response would be, "No it doesn't really look like it to me." Or you would say, "Inflation is really hurting the middle class the worst," and I would automatically say, "No, it doesn't really

hurt them that much." And then I would be forced to invent arguments to support my point of view. . . . Sometimes I got into ridiculous situations because I said no so automatically. I remember when we were driving home from skiing on really slippery roads and my friend who is really a very good driver said it would help if the two of them sat in back. Better weight distribution and that. . . . But I started naturally to say no so I had to insist that all three of us sit squeezed into the front seat of my little car, and I admit it was ridiculous but it was just my automatic negativism.

Psychologists use the term *functional autonomy* to describe traits that remain long after the purpose which they served has disappeared. People are exceedingly likely to have several functionally autonomous traits. Long ago, possibly during childhood or adolescence, it served them to be negativistic, aggressive, suspicious, or impatient. But now, years later, instead of helping them these traits may actually interfere with their growth. Yet most people, not having had the benefit of encounter or any analogous experience, are so unaware of themselves that they continue costly and maladaptive behavior that should have been dropped long ago.

Functionally autonomous traits are inappropriate in all areas of life but are perhaps most evident within marriage. In the continual intimacy of constant partnership, vestigial and intrusive personality habits grow more irritating and destructive with each passing day. Negativism, puritanism, temper tantrums, or brooding—any of these hangovers from childhood can totally destroy what might otherwise be a good relationship.

Here are some descriptions of typical personality changes stimulated by encounter experience.

Whenever Phil and I had any dispute, no matter how minor, I brooded. I was doing what I had learned to do as a child. I withdraw and remain silent and that was the end of that. . . . And it might well have ended our marriage . . . if I hadn't learned to talk, here. . . . Brooding was not serving me as an adult. . . . What I needed to do was communicate. . . . Now that we talk it is the difference between night and day. . . .

I had remained a Puritan till finally I saw that this was just still being a good little boy like my mother taught me. There is no more reason for me to still be a repressed little Boy Scout now than there is to kiss my mother good-night. . . . That might have been the thing to do as a child, but now I'm an adult. . . . What I think I got most out of this group is growing up and being sexually a man, not a little sheltered boy. . . . Lucille told me that she never realized I had it in me. She said we now have a lusty, passionate relationship, and it's so good it's like a guilty secret between us.

Conclusion

Like a good many graduates of growth encounter, I am in danger of sounding overenthusiastic about its effects and results. It is easy to be at least a little elated, for the changes evident in a few participants are fairly dramatic. They come to the group apprehensive and uncertain, often searching for feeling and identity. Their questions and inhibitions demonstrate their disorientation and alienation. But they finish by knowing themselves and their potential, experiencing love and excitement, and setting out in new creative directions. But I recognize that not everyone's growth is enhanced equally. While a few seem to take giant steps towards self-actualization, others leave the group knowing they have had a good and pleasant experience but gaining little else. These latter individuals are sometimes disappointed, for they may have expected to emerge totally renewed. This disparity is an inevitable consequence of any group experience; what is carried away by different members is not equal and cannot be guaranteed. Here too, however, I am optimistic, since even those who believe they have gained little may feel the effects of their experience later on. Often the group interaction leaves latent traces within the personality that lie dormant, waiting to show themselves slowly and subtly as circumstances permit.

At the other extreme, even the best participant, convinced

of his own momentous progress, may feel less rapturous about his actualization as time goes by. For some, encounter does bring about lifelong revelations and redirections that are profound and beneficial. For such people relations with spouse, family, friends, and employer are immeasurably improved, and their own abilities, talents, and goals are more visible and attainable than they ever thought possible. But for others, as the encounter experience recedes they "relapse" more and more into their old ways. Slowly the altruistic emotions that were kindled, the potentials that were sparked, sputter and die. Back in their customary environment, surrounded by conflict, misunderstanding, pressure, and frustration, and without the reinvigoration offered by the twice-weekly encounter sessions, they succumb bit by bit to their usual habits and routines.

But encounter need not end after twenty-five sessions. Those who "relapse" and even those who seem to have carried away permanent benefits may go on with other groups for more advanced experience. It is not generally necessary—and is often undesirable—for a group that has finished its predetermined number of sessions in, say, four months to recess and then continue. It is usually most beneficial if, after a year or so, those who feel a need or desire to go further seek another valid encounter group. Of course a valid group is not always distinguishable from a shabby imitation. Generally, if those who have had an initial growth experience want to continue, they should limit themselves to groups clearly described as suitable for those who have already had beginning experience and led by a specifically trained professional.

I am not advocating becoming an "encounter freak." As I pointed out in chapter 1, people who seek continual encounter gain little from growth groups and would often be better served by individual psychotherapy. Generally an advanced group is appropriate after a year or so, if a previous participant feels the need to go further or even just to recapture some of what he has learned previously. As a rule of thumb it is advisable, however, to limit the total number of encounter experiences after a second encounter to very brief occasional sessions, or to have more prolonged and intensive experiences with three, four, or even more years between. Encounter experiences that are generously spaced are not likely, in well-adapted individuals, to have any but rewarding effects.

Finally a word about the place and future of encounter in a very troubled world: I am not utopian enough to believe that if encounter were to spread to every nation and every level of society the result would be an affectionate and peaceful universe. It is very unlikely that encounter can change malevolence to kindness or replace powerful needs to dominate and control with charity and love. Those with the cruelest motives seldom if ever desire encounter or any other psychological interaction that might help them overcome their inclinations. Even more basic perhaps is the fact that the seriously destructive drives that may be causing so much of mankind's grief are probably too deeply rooted to be eradicated through encounter experience.

But whatever its limits, I do foresee valid encounter continuing and expanding. Our friends, relatives, and neighbors have found encounter an island of relative sanity and care in a fairly harsh world. Living lives increasingly characterized by distance and alienation, they have discovered a group that permits—in fact encourages—closeness and purpose. Through encounter, people have learned that at any age they can become more of what they are capable of being. Millions have found encounter a fulfilling experience, and I am certain that many times that number will find it a stimulant to growth in the years ahead.

Index

169

About the author—
Dr. Haas has been a professor of psychology at State University College, New Paltz, New York, since 1962. He also has taught at Bowling Green State University in Ohio. In recent years he has served as consulting clinical psychologist for a number of mental health agencies and facilities, including Matteawan State Hospital, The Children's Rehabilitation Center, Ulster County Mental Health Clinic, and St. Francis Hospital.

Dr. Haas is author of two books, *Understanding Ourselves and Others* and *Understanding Adjustment and Behavior,* a textbook being used in colleges throughout the United States and abroad. He has written over a dozen articles for professional psychology journals.

Dr. Haas received his doctorate in psychology from Pennsylvania State University.

GROWTH ENCOUNTER

A
Guide
for
Groups

Kurt Haas

Growth encounter, like other encounter-type experiences, is aimed at helping each participant bring out or maximize his or her capabilities . . . to stimulate self-development.

The technique involved is getting people together to respond honestly and openly with the help of an understanding and encouraging leader. In this way an individual may become better able to overcome social pressures, fears, guilt and self-doubt that may have minimized their capacity to have new experiences and to mature. Each group member is intent on exploring personal aptitudes, continuing his growth, and actualizing his potential.

Growth Encounter: A Guide for Groups provides complete, detailed instructions in the techniques and applications the author has found most successful in conducting or participating in a growth encounter group. It explains the preparation for the initial meeting of the participants, desirable personality characteristics for encounter participants, the processes involved in achieving participant interaction, the precautions to take, the pitfalls to anticipate, and the rewards to be sought.

Dr. Haas, a highly qualified professional, discusses the purpose of growth encounter; participants and the proper setting; guiding the group; techniques for starting; listening and talking reflecting feelings; questions, contradictions, and anger;